T0198617

AS QUIET AS A MOUSE

WHEN THERE'S NO ONE YOU CAN TRUST

MOLLY WILLIAMS

iUniverse, Inc.
New York   Bloomington

AS QUIET AS A MOUSE

Copyright © 2009 Molly Williams

The information, ideas, and suggestions in this book are not intended as a substitute for professional advice. Before following any suggestions contained in this book, you should consult your personal physician or mental health professional. Neither the author nor the publisher shall be liable or responsible for any loss or damage allegedly arising as a consequence of your use or application of any information or suggestions in this book.

iUniverse books may be ordered through booksellers or by contacting:

iUniverse
1663 Liberty Drive
Bloomington, IN 47403
www.iuniverse.com
1-800-Authors (1-800-288-4677)

Because of the dynamic nature of the Internet, any Web addresses or links contained in this book may have changed since publication and may no longer be valid. The views expressed in this work are solely those of the author and do not necessarily reflect the views of the publisher, and the publisher hereby disclaims any responsibility for them.

ISBN: 978-1-4401-8238-9 (pbk)
ISBN: 978-1-4401-8236-5 (cloth)
ISBN: 978-1-4401-8237-2 (ebk)

Printed in the United States of America

iUniverse rev. date: 10/14/2009

Contents

AUTHOR BIOGRAPHY

When I was just a young woman, a mother of three small children, something happened to me. Someone or something took over my mind and took over my body and I had no control over what was happening to me. The doctor diagnosed me as having bipolar illness, a genetic disorder, a chemical imbalance in my brain. He could call it anything he wanted but all I heard was "mental illness." I knew things weren't right with me. I had always known, since I was a small child, and I knew exactly who the people were who caused it. I had carried bitterness toward them my whole life. But what did I do about it? Did I tell on them? Did I try to hurt them back? No, I took their guilt on and turned it into my shame. I tucked that shame deep down inside of me so no one would know and I let it eat away at me until it finally destroyed me and attempted to destroy my family too. Now it's time to let go. It's time to place blame where blame is due.

INTRODUCTION

I was thirty years old when I was diagnosed with bipolar illness. Overnight, everything about me changed. I became a completely different person from the inside out. It was as though another woman, completely opposite from me, had taken over my body and I had no control over the things she was doing. Not only my personality changed but also my appearance, my mannerisms, my dress, my spending habits, my friendships, and my mothering abilities. Most of all, it changed the way people thought of me.

I had always been very shy, quiet, and mildly depressed, and I had always hated myself. A lot had happened to me when I was a child that I blamed myself for, and because of it I had withdrawn into a shell and there were very few people I allowed inside. Before the illness hit me, I was a plain Jane. I wore plain clothes, my hair was long and straight, and I never wore makeup or jewelry. I did everything I could possibly do to keep from drawing attention to myself.

When this new person took over my body, something wonderful happened to me. For the first time in my life, I felt completely happy, and for the first time in my life, I was actually happy to be me. There was nothing I couldn't accomplish if I set my mind to it, and although I knew something unusual was happening to me, I also knew that whatever it was, it wasn't going to last long. I had to make the best of it while I could.

At night, I never slept. My nervous system was on fast speed. I stayed up to all hours cleaning the house, painting the walls, or working on one of the many projects I had started but never seemed to finish. Before the illness hit me, I had weighed 125 lbs. In a very short period of time, I was down to 97 lbs. I just didn't feel the need to eat. I was enjoying life too much to slow down. I started wearing a lot of makeup. I curled and teased my hair up and dressed as provocatively as I could. Before the illness hit me, I would have never imagined cheating on my husband. I loved him and my three little girls so much, and even though I knew what I was doing was wrong, I had no control over my actions. Everything I did felt like the right thing to do.

My family, my friends, and my co-workers were totally bewildered by what was happening to me. I had changed from this shy, quiet, boring young mother to this happy, talkative, hyper woman who was over the top with self-confidence and ideas. People liked me more. I could feel it. For as long as I could remember, I had carried so much guilt and shame inside of me and I had tried very hard to hide it, and so when this new person surfaced, all of that disappeared. I would do anything to keep it that way. But time has a way of changing things. It just wasn't meant to be.

After weeks of begging and pleading and trying to convince me that something was wrong, my husband finally talked me into going to the doctor. What he didn't tell me was that he was taking me to a psychiatrist whom he had already met with, and because he knew I would object, I was there simply to be transported to a mental hospital in Nashville.

After one session with the doctor, whom I will refer to as Dr. J., I was diagnosed with bipolar illness, and I was in a manic state of the illness. The doctor explained to me that the bipolar illness was caused by a chemical imbalance in my brain. I stayed in the hospital for three weeks while they started me on a series of medications that they hoped would level me out, one of which was lithium. The medication made me stiff. It was hard to walk, I couldn't turn my head and I could hardly move my arms and legs. My vision was so blurred that I could hardly see in front of me. I hated my husband for doing this to me. I couldn't understand why he didn't want me to be happy, and I made the decision to leave him when I was released from the hospital. But that prospect didn't fly with Dr. J. He would release me on one condition: that I go home to my husband and children. I wanted out of that hospital so much that I had no choice but to agree to his conditions.

Once I got home, I started improving and after three weeks I started becoming my old self again, the self I hated. All the great things I felt, not only about myself but also about my life in general disappeared. All that was left was embarrassment and humiliation. Everyone thought I had gone crazy, and the thing is that they were right. It had been complete craziness. The manic symptoms subsided, but I remained in a mild state of depression and came to the realization that nothing would cure that. It's just who I was.

I started seeing Dr. J. on a regular basis, and when I started telling him about my childhood, he asked me to start writing journals about the things that had happened. He explained that it was a form of transference and that writing my memories down on paper would be a form of release and, hopefully, some sort of closure. I wish I could say that it worked. It didn't. What the writing did, however, was help me remember things I had not thought of in a long time and also things I had blocked from my memory completely. At times, I became so emotional that I had to stop writing and put the journals away for a while.

Dr. J. had told me early on that bipolar illness was genetic, but no one else in my family had ever been diagnosed with it. I seemed to be the first, and even though I carried the gene, I was told that it might never have surfaced had I not been exposed to an extreme amount of stress. Deep down inside, I knew why I had the illness, and it wasn't because it was genetic.

Once Dr. J. started reading my journals, he was astonished that the illness had not surfaced when I was very young. In fact, he was surprised that I had not committed suicide by the time I was fourteen years old.

"Why didn't you tell your parents what was happening to you?" was his question.

"My parents didn't get along" I told him. "They fought all the time. I didn't want to cause more problems than there already were. I hated the fighting and I certainly didn't want them fighting because of me."

And then I answered him with this, "Besides, they probably wouldn't have believed me anyway, and if they did, they would have blamed me for everything that happened." That answer in itself summed everything up.

After the last journal was written, Dr. J. insisted that I tell my family everything that had happened to me, but I adamantly refused. Every since I had been diagnosed with the mental illness, my family had shunned me. They treated me as though my illness were contagious. To tell them everything that had happened would surely send them over the edge. I had never wanted anybody to know. I had kept the secrets to myself for all those years and I saw no purpose in telling them now.

After five years of therapy, however, I gave in to Dr. J.'s demands. My condition had not improved like he had hoped. I would slip from my normal state of mind into a depressed state that would sometimes spiral into mania. It felt like I was living the life of three different women, and there was nothing I could do to stop any one of them from making her appearance.

Most of the time I was myself, always mildly depressed but trying my best to appear happy and normal; but I was never happy. I was always yearning for something better even though my life was as good as it could possibly get. I had a husband who loved me, three adoring children, a large and close-knit family, and close friends. But it was never enough. I just couldn't be satisfied.

Then something would happen to make the severely depressed side of me appear. For weeks, sometimes months, I would be so sad that I could hardly get out of the bed. I kept the curtains pulled and the lights off and wanted no one around me. All I did was cry. I would go back to the doctor and he would start me on a new regimen of medication hoping the depression would subside; sometimes it worked, sometimes not.

Then, out of nowhere and for no reason, the manic side of me would come out. She made her appearance much less often than the normal and depressed states, but when she did, it would destroy everything I had tried so hard to build up. I had spent my whole life trying to be a good person, a person whom people thought highly of and a person people wanted for their friend. More than anything, I wanted to be a good wife and have a happy home. I wanted to be the best mother for my children. I wanted them to know how much I loved them, and I wanted them to know that no matter what, they could always trust me to be there for them. When the manic side of me appeared, however, everything I had worked for went down the drain. Although I loved who I was when it took me over, it only turned people away from me, and their feelings about me changed. When my normal self would reappear, it would take months, maybe years, before I would feel people warm up to me again. Finally, when I agreed to tell my family about my childhood, I did it only because I agreed with Dr. J. I was carrying too much guilt inside of me, and just writing about what happened wasn't enough. Mama had already died; out of everyone in my life, she was the one person who knew something was wrong with me, but she didn't dare admit it. She had loved me—I was sure of that—but she was a fragile soul herself. She didn't have it in her to help me. I had never felt sure of Daddy's love, and so it wouldn't bother me to tell him. All I could possibly hope for is that he would listen to me and try his best to help me understand what happened and why.

When I finally told Daddy what had happened, the reaction was not what I had hoped for, but it was what I expected. In so many words, Daddy told me simply to keep my mouth shut. "People don't need to know what happens in our family," he said. "Besides, it happened such a long time ago. Just forget about it." The tone of his voice was anger and the look in his eyes disgust, so much that I had to look away from him.

It didn't stop me, however, from saying, "I wish I could forget about it, Daddy. Don't you see that this is what's made me sick? I've kept these secrets for thirty years because I never felt I had anybody to help me, and now I see that I still don't. But don't you worry, Daddy. I won't tell anybody else." The conversation ended. My instinct had been right all along. There was no one to help me, not then and not now.

I had been in therapy with Dr. J. for years when he approached me about turning the journals into a book.

"You have so much to tell," he said, "and if you could help change the life of just one child, wouldn't you?"

"Of course I would," I told him. "But how?"

"Say your journals were published, what would your message be?"

The answer to that was simple. No matter how much a child feels it, when something horrible happens to them at the hands of someone bad, they need to know that it's not their fault. The number-one job adults have in life should be protecting their children, but they take that safety for granted. They get so caught up in their own lives that a lot of times they fail to do their job. All they really have to do is watch and listen and, most importantly, instill trust in their children. Every child needs to know and feel that someone cares about them and that no matter what someone is there to help and protect them. They have to feel that they matter to someone.

I don't know what will happen if my journals are published. I don't know how it will affect my family. What I do know is that when you experience the things I experienced, something good must come out of it and, hopefully, some sort of healing. All I can hope for is that my journals will serve the purpose that is intended. It's said that the things that happen to us happen for a reason. Hopefully, what happened to me did happen for a reason.

Recently, in my Bible study class, we studied a book written by James W. Moore titled *There's a Hole in Your Soul That Only GOD Can Fill*. In it, he wrote, "In recent years, psychologists have emphasized how important the early years are. Our personalities, attitudes, values, habits, principles, self-esteem and even our I-Q are shaped so powerfully by what happens to us in the first few years of life."

I have two brothers who grew up to be well-adjusted, successful, happy people.

As for me, I never had a chance.

UNCLE TEA

My family lived in Portland, Tennessee, a small farming community north of Nashville on the Tennessee-Kentucky line. My small world consisted of Mama and Daddy, my two older brothers, Paul and Tommy, and my baby sister, Kathy. We lived in a large, gray shingle house on an enormous farm. My grandparents, Mammie and Papa, lived down the road about a mile from us in a small, four-room log cabin that Papa and Daddy had built when Daddy was eleven years old.

I loved living on the farm. It was such a wonderful experience and one that I wish most kids could have at some point in their lifetime. There was no computer, no Internet, or anything else to occupy our minds inside the house. There was just too much fun to be had outside. My brothers and I were up at the crack of dawn; we ate breakfast and then headed out the door to help Daddy feed the chickens and the cows. We played in the hayloft down at the barn or we waded in the creek down in the wooded area back behind our house. When Daddy would let us, we rode on the tractor with him while he plowed up the fields to plant his crops, and sometimes at lunch, my brothers and I would ride in the bed of his truck to the little country store near our house. There, Daddy would buy a loaf of bread, a pack of bologna, and RC Colas for everyone and we'd sit under the shade of a tree and eat. My memory of the farm is the only time in my life that I remember feeling completely happy, free, and content.

The only memory I wish I could forget, however, was Mama and Daddy's relationship. They fought constantly. All they did was argue and scream, mostly over money. The fighting usually started at breakfast and continued well into the night until they finally went to bed and fell asleep. If Mama and Daddy were anywhere near each other, they were fighting.

Although I loved my life on the farm, our home was unhappy and seemed to be filled only with hate. When I was at home, I either stayed in my room with the door shut or, if the weather allowed, outside as far away from the house as I could so I couldn't hear the screaming.

The only happy place I did know was my grandparents' house, and that was because of Mammie's rule. There was to be no fighting in her house, and Mama and Daddy understood that they had to abide by her rule or they were not welcome. Mammie was one of the most important people in my life. She was so full of love and laughter, and one of the fondest memories I have of Mammie was her cooking. Chicken was served up at almost every meal, freshly killed chicken. Mammie would grab up one of the chickens walking around the yard, take it by the neck, and twist it round and round until its head came off. If it didn't come off easy enough, she laid the chicken on the tree stump right outside the back door, took an axe, and chopped its head off. There lay the chicken's head, blood dripping from his neck, while the rest of its body ran around the yard wild and frantic. Finally, after a minute or so, it would fall to the ground dead. Then she plucked all its feathers off, cut it into pieces, and fried it up for dinner. You would think it would be impossible to eat the chicken after watching how it died, but you couldn't not eat Mammie's chicken. It was out of this world. Besides feeding the whole family on Sundays, Mammie served a hot, full-course meal every day to the five or six farmhands who worked for Papa. The cabin was always filled with laughter and happiness, and I hated having to go home.

My feelings, however, about the cabin and everything else in my life changed one day. Any happiness, contentment, or feeling of security that I had known ended there one day when I was five years old.

It was spring and strawberry season at our house, the most exciting time of the year, more so than Christmas. At least I thought so.

I had turned five in January and was to start school in the fall. The Mexicans had come in from other states to pick our strawberries. They would be there for at least six weeks or until every strawberry was picked, crated, and shipped off to the buyers. Not just the men came in. With them, they brought their whole families—wives, children, and grandparents. It was the only time of the year when we would have children to play with. The only problem was that not one of them could speak English. The great thing about children, though, is that they can usually communicate without saying a word.

For that short period of time during strawberry season, the fighting between Mama and Daddy ceased. Not only were they too busy, but our money was plentiful.

Today, my dad has apartments for the Mexicans to live in that have electricity and running water. Back then, the Mexicans slept in the barns. The women hung handmade quilts between the stalls to make bedrooms for each family. Sometimes, Mama let us go down to the barns at suppertime to eat with the Mexicans. They sat around a big open fire, ate beans and tortillas, sang songs, laughed, and sometimes even danced. They led very simple lives, and it seemed that they only lived from day to day, but they were truly happy. I sat and watched them and I wished so hard that Mama and Daddy were happy; if they had been, maybe it would have extended to us. I guess it just wasn't meant to be, but at least, for six weeks or more every summer, my brothers and I got to witness true happiness.

Every day during picking season, Mama worked at the wagons handing out tickets to the Mexicans for each quart of berries they picked. One day, instead of taking me with her, she dropped me off to stay with Mammie while she went to the fields. I was always happy to go to Mammie's, but that day, I didn't want to stay. Uncle Tea was visiting her, just as he did every summer. He was Mammie's nephew. Not only was he scary looking, but he never talked. He just stared. Mama and Daddy had laughed at him and said he looked like a "black crow." They said that he "wasn't right" and that Mammie felt sorry for him. He had never been married and had no children. He still lived with his parents, and I found out years later that he worked for the Davidson County sheriff's office, in what aspect I don't know. As much as I loved being at Mammie's, I didn't want to go if he was there. I was scared to death of him and did everything I could to keep my distance and avoid his stares.

That particular day when Mama dropped me off, Papa had come in from the fields and told Mammie he needed her help. Mammie never worked the fields. She was too busy preparing the noontime meal. As soon as she started getting ready to go help Papa, I got frantic. I followed her around grabbing at her skirt tails, crying and begging her to take me with her. The whole time, she kept telling me to stop and telling me, "Uncle Tea will take good care of you." I couldn't believe that she was about to leave me with him, and as she started walking out the door, I ran to her and put my arms around her waist and begged, "Please Mammie, don't leave me!"

She took me by the shoulders, pushed me away, and told Uncle Tea to hold me. "I'll be right back," she said. "Uncle Tea won't hurt you." She handed me over to him and walked out the door, shutting it behind her. I watched as she walked to her car, got in, and drove away, and I couldn't believe it. She was leaving me. She had to know how scared I was of him, but obviously she didn't care.

As soon as her car disappeared, I jerked away from Uncle Tea, ran to the den, and turned the TV on. I sat down in front of it on the floor with my back to him, and although I pretended to watch the TV, my concentration was on Uncle Tea. Where was he and what was he doing? I knew he was there in the room with me, but where? Suddenly, he walked past me to the window and looked out. He turned, stepped in front of me, and turned the TV off. He reached down, took me by the arm, and pulled me up. He was not gentle, and his voice was stern. "Come on, Molly," he said. "Let's play a game."

He told me to stand still while he went into the bathroom. As I watched him leave the room, I started shaking all over and wanted to run but was afraid of what he'd do if I did. I heard him turn the water on. Then, he came back into the room with a towel and a wet washrag. He placed the towel on the floor near the window and made me stand on it. He made me turn around while he unbuttoned the tiny buttons on the back of my dress. He pulled my dress over my head. The whole time, I kept trying to pull away from him and cried for him to stop, but it only made him angry. He took me by my shoulders, shook me, and said, "Shut up and be still."

Tears rolled down onto my cheeks. I was afraid to fight him. He proceeded to pull my panties down to the floor and over my feet, and there I stood, totally naked. You can't imagine the humiliation I felt, and I guess you wouldn't think that a small child five years old could feel humiliation, but I did. I remember my heart beating so fast that I thought it would jump out of my chest. He made me spread my legs apart. I started pushing at him, and he grabbed both of my arms and pulled them behind me, holding them with one hand so I couldn't move. Then he did the unthinkable. He put his head down between my legs and started kissing my vagina. I felt so nasty. I couldn't believe this was happening to me. He started digging his long, dirty fingernails up into my vagina, and I felt the skin tear away. It felt like he had a knife and was cutting me over and over again up inside my stomach. It's hard to describe what I was feeling and the fear I felt. It's impossible. He pressed his lips against my face, and I smelled his hot, nasty breath. As much as I could, I jerked and tried to get away from him, but the more I did, the madder he got. He pulled his finger out of me and grabbed my cheeks, squeezing them together and forcing me to look at him. "Be still," he said. "I'm not hurting you." I cried hard but did not say a word. He resumed digging his fingers up inside of me and I couldn't hold it. I peed on myself. The urine ran down my legs and onto the towel below. Uncle Tea screamed, "Look what you've done! You're nasty now." He wiped me with the washrag, and when he did, the rag was bloody and so was the towel below. His disgust, however, didn't slow him down or make him want to stop. The whole time Uncle Tea was raping me, he kept glancing out the window for Mammie or anybody else to come down the driveway. I was too small to see out the window, but I could hear if a car was coming. It didn't.

When Uncle Tea stopped digging his fingers into me, he said, "Now it's time for you to make Uncle Tea feel good." He unbuckled his belt, unzipped his pants, and pulled them and his underwear down to the floor. There, in front of me, at face level, was his penis. He started pulling on it with one hand while holding my hands behind my back with the other. Then he let my hands go but held the back of my head. As he tried to force his penis into my mouth, I gritted my teeth, but he grabbed me again by the cheeks and squeezed me so hard that my face hurt. "Open your mouth," he screamed. He forced my mouth open with his fingers and pushed his penis inside. "Pretend it's a cherry sucker," he said.

It had been in there only a second or two when I gagged and bit down. He jerked it out of my mouth and smacked my cheek. He grabbed my head between his hands and started squeezing it. "Don't bite me," he screamed. "Suck it." It felt like he was crushing my head, and I went limp like a rag doll. There was ringing in my ears, and my heart was pounding as fast as it could. Then I realized that it didn't matter what I did, how loud I screamed, or how hard I fought—there was no one coming to help me.

As I stood there, I thought about Mama and Mammie. I had begged both of them not to leave me. The thing I remember is that I hadn't just begged. I had screamed in terror. They had to know how scared I was, but obviously they didn't care. I wondered why they didn't love me. I had tried to be a good girl. I couldn't imagine what I had done to cause this.

Finally Uncle Tea pulled his penis out of my mouth and covered it with the wet washrag. He made terrible sounds. I thought I had hurt him and was scared of what he'd do to me next. It was as though I was waiting for the inevitable.

Finally he pulled his pants up and told me not to move. He walked away into the bathroom and I just stood, naked, on top of the towel. My whole body was numb. I didn't know how to feel. When he came back into the den, he was fully dressed. He washed my face with a wet washrag he brought from the bathroom. Then he made me spread my legs apart and he washed between my vagina and my legs. With nervous hands, he pulled my panties up, pulled my dress down over my head, turned me around, and buttoned my dress. And then he said, "It won't hurt the next time, Molly. I love you." He said, "You should have been my little girl."

After he made sure everything was put away and things were as they should be, he walked over to the window, looked out, turned, and walked back to me. I stood like a tiny statue. I didn't know what to do or how to feel. He took me by the hand and we walked through the living room and outside to the front porch. There he lifted me up to the porch swing, sat down beside me, and pulled me close to him, putting his arm around me.

"You can't tell anybody about this," he said. "If you do, everybody will think you're nasty. They won't love you anymore. If they find out, you'll get a bad spanking. Do you want a spanking?"

I shook my head "no" but never answered him. I was so scared of getting a spanking. I had never gotten one, but I had seen Tommy get plenty of them. Tommy was always getting into trouble. Daddy would go out back behind our house and pull a limb from the cherry tree. He would pull all the leaves off it until it was stripped clean; then he'd stripe Tommy's legs five or six times with it until they bled and Tommy would cry. I always cried too. I think it hurt me as much as it did Tommy. I knew I could never tell what Uncle Tea did to me, not so much because of the spanking I would get but because he was right—I had been nasty. Mama and Daddy wouldn't want me around anymore. They wouldn't love me anymore. Most of the time, I felt that they didn't love me anyway. If they did, they surely wouldn't have let Uncle Tea hurt me.

As I sat in the swing with Uncle Tea and waited, I thought about what he had said, that he "loved me," that "I should have been his little girl," and what I thought to myself was this: "If that's the way a Daddy loves you, then I'm glad my Daddy doesn't love me."

While we waited for Mammie to come home, Uncle Tea started singing "Old MacDonald Had a Farm E-I-E-I-O." Over and over again he sang, verse by verse. Although I despise the song, I always sang it to my children because they loved it. But for me, it's only a reminder of what happened that dreadful day.

As I sat and waited for Mammie to come home, I told myself, "Never again will I let him hurt me. I'll never let him get close enough. If Mama and Mammie won't stop him, then I will."

After that day, I built a wall up around me. I lost all trust in the people I depended on to protect me, and I knew that if anyone hurt me ever again, then it would be no one's fault but my own. I was just five years old, and if I had been a happy child before that day, I was never happy again.

It was quite a while before Mammie's car came down the driveway. As she walked from the driveway to the house and up to the porch, she hollered "Ya'll doing okay?"

"Oh yeah," Uncle Tea hollered back. "We're doing just fine."

She walked up on the porch, looked at me, and said, "Molly, see,

I told you Uncle Tea would take good care of you, didn't I?" I didn't look at her and I never said a word. There were no tears. There was no emotion. If Mammie wondered at all if anything was wrong with me, she never even asked. She just opened the door and walked back into the house.

"Come on," she said. "I'll fix ya'll some dinner."

Still I sat there. Uncle Tea got up from the swing, turned to me, put his finger to his lips, and whispered, "Remember, Molly, it's our secret."

When he went inside and closed the door, I climbed down from the swing and ran to the other side of the house, the side where no one could see me. I sat down next to the house, pulled my knees to my chest, and cried. My vagina and my stomach hurt so badly, and so did my face where he had grabbed me. I stayed there until Mammie called me in for dinner. I sat at the table with my head bowed both in fear and also in shame, and although Mammie tried to persuade me to eat, I couldn't. I felt too sick. When Mama came to pick me up, I never went to her, and when she was ready to leave, I walked to the car, opened the back door, got in, and shut it. Mama and Mammie had betrayed me. I knew I could never trust them again.

I hid in my room that night and came out only to eat supper. I was determined not to let anyone see what pain I was in. When I took my clothes off that night to take a bath, there was blood in my panties. I locked the bathroom door, and even at Mama's insistence, I wouldn't let her in. I couldn't let her see the blood. After I bathed and put my pajamas on, I cracked the bathroom door to make sure no one was there and slipped out the back door. I wrapped the bloody panties up and threw them in the trash can, careful to cover them up with the other garbage. Daddy would burn the trash the next day and all signs of what Uncle Tea had done to me would be gone. No one would ever know.

For a few days, I continued to bleed and I continued to hide it. I stuffed toilet paper up inside my vagina so I wouldn't bleed into my panties. The pain was terrible, and I still don't know how I hid that. It amazes me, as do many things about my parents, that they couldn't see that something was terribly wrong with me. If they even thought it, they never asked. Not once. Every day I just went through the motions. I did what I was told and said as little as possible to anyone. I didn't want anyone to talk to me either. I was afraid that if they did, I would cry. If I felt like I was going to cry, I hid. When Mama and Daddy fought, if the weather didn't permit me to go outside, I hid in the back of my closet with my knees pulled to my chest and my hands over my ears. The fear and the tension in our house took over my mind and my existence.

That summer went by and I wasn't alone with Uncle Tea again. Maybe I had begged my way out of it. I don't remember. However, on one occasion, my family and I were at Mammie's for Sunday dinner, and when Mammie called everyone to the table, somehow I was seated next to him. I sat in my chair as far to the other side as possible so as not to touch him, but Uncle Tea put his arm across the back of my chair and rested his hand on my shoulder. When he did, I got up and ran as fast as I could out the back door. I heard Mama say, "Molly, come back in here and sit down and eat. What's wrong with you?"

I just kept running, and I heard Daddy laugh and say, "I don't think she likes you, Tea." He was laughing. Everyone was laughing. They thought it was funny. They were teasing him. At the driveway, I waited and I watched. If he came outside, I would run, all the way home if I had to. Mammie came to the back door and then went back inside. She came back out with a plate of food for me. She called me to the big tree stump toward the front of the house, and there I ate my plate of food with my eyes constantly pinned on the back door.

I managed somehow to evade Uncle Tea the rest of that summer, but every spring after that year, rather than being like most children who looked forward to spring and the end of the school year, all I thought about was, "It's spring. He's coming."

Kathy was one year old when Uncle Tea raped me. Not only did I do everything I could to protect myself when we had to be around him, but I took it on myself to protect Kathy too. There was a difference, though. Mama never left Kathy with Mammie, or anyone else for that matter. Wherever Mama went, she always took Kathy with her. I was jealous of that, but I was also relieved. I couldn't imagine Uncle Tea doing to her what he did to me, and if for one second I thought he might, then I knew I would have to tell.

The last time that I was ever left with Uncle Tea was when I was eight years old. Once again I pleaded, begged, and even cried to both Mama and Mammie not to leave me. It was like an instant replay, but this time, as soon as Mammie walked out of the house to her car, I ran outside and to the back of the house and hid. When she was out of sight, Uncle Tea came out of the house and called for me, "Molly, come inside, come on now." I knew what he wanted, and I wasn't about to go inside. I didn't answer him, and then heard him say, "Oh, so you want to play hide and seek?" He was coming after me.

I watched for him from behind a tree, and when I saw him come around the corner of the house, I ran to the next corner and watched for him again. There he came, not running, just walking slowly toward me, calling for me, "Don't be afraid, Molly, I'm not going to hurt you."

That's what he had told me that first day—"The next time it won't hurt"—and that's all I could think about. I couldn't let him catch me. I ran as fast as I could to the front of the house and out to the driveway watching for him to follow me. When he rounded the front corner of the house, he saw me and started walking toward the driveway. That's when I started screaming, "I'll tell Mammie! I will!"

I started running up the driveway toward the fields when I heard him yell, "Molly, stop! I won't hurt you. I'll sit right here on the porch. I promise. Come back."

I turned to see him walk up on the porch and sit in the swing. As bad as I wanted to keep running, I stopped and sat down in the driveway. What he had said to me that day had stayed with me every day since. "You've been nasty," he had said. "No one will love you anymore." As bad as I wanted someone to help me, I didn't want them to know what had happened. I didn't think they loved me anyway, not since Kathy was born. What would they do if they found out? I was afraid they would send me away.

I sat in the driveway and watched for Mammie to come home, never taking my eyes away from Uncle Tea. He sat in the swing and never took his eyes off of me either. He just sat there with that cold stare and, I'm sure, wondered if I was going to tell on him. As I watched him, I started asking myself questions. What would happen if, when Mammie came back, she saw me sitting there in the driveway? Would she ask why I was there? Would she be curious enough and concerned enough to realize that something was wrong? I answered that question myself. "No, she wouldn't." Mama and Daddy always talked about how much she loved Uncle Tea because, as they had said, he "wasn't right," and I'm sure she thought he couldn't hurt a fly. But he did. He hurt me. The physical damage would heal with time, but the damage he did to me mentally would be lifelong. I loved Mama and Mammie so much, but they had let me down. My trust in them, in anyone, was gone. That too would affect me for the rest of my life.

It was a long time before I saw Mammie's car coming down the driveway. I stood up and waited for her to circle the driveway and park the car; then I ran to her and grabbed her around the waist, holding back the tears that were choking me. She hugged me back but never asked if anything was wrong. I glanced over at Uncle Tea. He was smiling. He knew our secret was safe. He knew I would never tell.

When I was nine years old, we moved away from the farm. I never saw Uncle Tea again. When I grew up, got married, and had my three children, I took them to see Mammie and Papa often, but before we'd ever leave our house, I always called her, and if Uncle Tea was there, we didn't go.

When I was twenty-four, Daddy called one night to give me the news. Uncle Tea had died. He told me when the funeral was and what time he would pick me up for the drive to Nashville. I told him I wasn't going. His response was, "What do you mean you're not going? I know you never liked him, but he's family. You have to go to his funeral."

With a firm voice and short and to the point, I told him, "I'm not going, Daddy," and when he asked me why not, I gave no excuse. Again, very simply, I told him, "I'm not going." I was a grown woman. Finally my life was in my control. He couldn't make me go.

After he hung up, I went outside and sat on the patio by myself. I cried long and hard, but it wasn't because I was sad. My wish had finally come true. It was over. I wouldn't have to worry about him anymore. He'd never be close enough to hurt me again. I wish I could say that my fear ended with his death, but one question always stayed in the back of my mind. What if he hurt another child the way he hurt me? I wasn't the only one. I was sure of that. Pedophiles don't stop with one. They don't stop until they're caught. So how many more children did he hurt because I didn't tell?

I'm still amazed that I was that tiny, five-year-old girl who was brutally raped and who was in so much pain for days and days after but still managed somehow to take care of herself and hide what had happened from everyone around her. I was scared to death to tell the only people in my life whom I depended on, but being totally honest, I didn't hide it that well. The signs were there. All they had to do was look at me.

Many years after Papa died, Mammie moved up to the main road in a small white shingle house. After that I never went back in the cabin again, but the haunting memories of what happened there are always with me. The move to the little house up on the main road was good for Mammie, but nobody will ever know how good the move was for me.

In her living room, Mammie had a tall stand up shelf against the wall, and on it sat every family picture she could fit in. There on the shelf that was at eye-level sat a full-size eight-by-ten picture of Uncle Tea. He was standing in front of a Davidson County sheriff's car.

No matter where I sat in that room, it was hard to avoid that cold stare of his eyes and the crow-like face Mama and Daddy had laughed about so often.

One Sunday, not very long after Mammie's move, I took my three little girls to her house for dinner. While she was in the kitchen busy frying up chicken, I went into the living room, took the picture of Uncle Tea, and put it in the trunk of my car. The picture stayed in my trunk for weeks and kept haunting me until finally, one day while my husband and children were gone, I took the picture from my trunk. I removed it from the frame and stared at it for the longest time. For ten minutes of sick pleasure, this man had stolen my childhood from me. Not only had he hurt me physically and mentally, but I felt like he had destroyed my soul. I took the picture outside, struck a match, and watched it burn. As his face faded into ashes, I prayed that he was burning in hell, and somehow I knew he was.

KATHY

Kathy was my little sister. She was born when I was four years old. From the very first day Mama brought her home from the hospital, I felt like she was mine, my very own baby doll. Mama was good about letting me help her with Kathy. Together we changed her diapers, bathed her, and dressed her, and at dinnertime I sat next to her so I could help feed her. Every night I sat in the rocking chair beside Mama while she read to Kathy and rocked her to sleep, and when she grew old enough to come out of the baby bed, she slept in my bed with me. Kathy made me feel loved and complete, the way no one else did.

Before Kathy was born, I had never really seen Daddy show anybody affection. He roughhoused with my brothers and seemed to enjoy the time he spent with them, but he had very little to do with me. He always seemed to be so tired and mad and unhappy, but when Kathy was born, she brought something out in him. The first thing he did when he came in from the fields was to pick her up, throw her in the air, and cuddle her. If he ever talked to me or read to me or kissed me goodnight, I have no memory of it. I am looking at a picture of Daddy now. He's down on the floor on his hands and knees riding Kathy on his back while I'm sitting over on the couch just watching and wishing that he loved me too. I didn't want to be, but I was so jealous of Kathy. That jealousy would be something I would regret for many years to come.

The more Kathy grew, the more beautiful she became. She had

milky white skin, rosy cheeks, red lips, and dark hair. We both wore our hair long with bangs, and from time to time people would tell Mama we looked like twins.

Kathy had turned four years old in January and I had turned eight. April had come, the Mexicans had arrived, and strawberry season was in full force. One day, Mama sent word to Daddy in the fields. He was to come home quick. Kathy was missing.

The first thing that ran through my mind was Uncle Tea. Kathy had been just one year old when Uncle Tea molested me, and I was always so scared that Uncle Tea would get hold of her. I took the job of protecting her on myself. But Uncle Tea hadn't come to Mammie's for the summer yet. I knew the only other thing it could be was the Mexicans. What if one of them got her? How could I have let her slip away? I was more frantic than anyone to find her. We looked everywhere we knew to look inside the house and we covered every piece of ground outside, but Kathy was nowhere to be found. Mama was frantic and cried uncontrollably, and Daddy ran from room to room calling for Kathy. When we had given up all hope of finding her and everyone got quiet, Daddy heard a small whimpering sound. It came from underneath Mama and Daddy's bed. There she was, back in the corner, drawn up in a knot like a small kitten. When Daddy was finally able to pull her from beneath the bed, she grabbed her stomach and told him, "My belly hurts, Daddy." Mama thought that it was just something she had eaten and the stomachache would go away, but Kathy stayed sick for days. Finally Mama took her to the local doctor who referred her to a specialist in Nashville. The diagnosis was short and to the point: Kathy had cancer.

Every week, Mama took her to St. Thomas Hospital in Nashville where she took cobalt treatments. My brothers and I always went with them to the hospital, and after her treatments, we went to Centennial Park for a picnic and we fed the ducks. The trip away from the farm was something rarely done. It was a special treat for Paul and Tommy and me. All Kathy could do, however, was lie on the blanket and watch. She was too sick and too weak to play. Always, when she came home from having the treatments, she was lifeless and had to be put to bed, and after a while Kathy wasn't able to play with me anymore. She had to be carried everywhere because she was too weak to walk. I found myself filled with anger. I was too young to understand what cancer was, and I didn't understand why Mama kept taking Kathy to the doctor, knowing how sick it was making her. I didn't understand why the doctor wanted to hurt her. I didn't understand any of it, but then nobody took the time to explain anything to me. Every day I sat on the bed with Kathy and watched as she slowly drifted away.

Not long after Kathy started taking the treatments, Mama got the scissors and I watched as she cut all of Kathy's hair off. I had been noticing that her hair was coming out when I brushed it, but I thought Mama cut it because she didn't want to take the time to wash it and fix it, and I begged her to let me do it. I promised that I would keep it washed and fixed, but Mama cut it off anyway. Now her hair was like Paul and Tommy's—short like a boy's. She didn't look the same after that. She was nothing but skin and bones, and her skin was ashen and her eyes hollow. She looked like a tiny skeleton lying in the bed.

Our house had always been so busy and full of life, but after Kathy became sick, everything changed. Everyone tiptoed around and whispered, scared to make a sound that might wake her up. Mama and Daddy cried all the time. Paul and Tommy either stayed in their room with the door shut or they stayed outside. I was forbidden to go into Kathy's room for fear it would wake her up, but I never ventured very far from her room. I sat outside her door and waited patiently to be told I could go in, and when I knew no one would see me, I buried my face in my hands and cried. Sometimes I waited at her door for hours, listening for her to make her whimpering sound that told me she was awake and I could go in.

Daddy went out to work every morning on the farm, and as soon as he came back to the house, he went straight to Kathy and held her in his arms. I watched as the tears rolled down his cheeks. I felt so sad for him, and I wished over and over again that I could take her place. He wouldn't be so sad if it was me who was sick.

Mama and Daddy never told me how sick Kathy really was. What they kept telling me was, "Kathy's getting better. It won't be long before she's all well." I believed them.

Kathy had been sick all summer, and the treatments weren't making her any better. Finally Mama took her to the doctor one day, and she didn't bring Kathy back home with her. Kathy went into the hospital to stay. That night, Mama came home and packed her bags, and instead of being totally honest with me, she told me, "Kathy will get well faster in the hospital, and soon she'll be coming home."

I remember feeling this sudden rush of happiness come over me. I knew I would miss Mama and Kathy, but if staying in the hospital for a few days would make Kathy well, then I was glad she went. I didn't even mind that Mama was leaving me to go with her.

With Mama and Kathy gone, the house was more quiet than ever. My brothers and Daddy were always out in the fields, and I spent most of my days alone, just wandering the house. I was consumed with sadness. Although I was just eight and no one had explained Kathy's illness to me, I knew something wasn't right, and as much as I wanted to believe she was getting well, like they were telling me, a dreaded fear stayed with me and I couldn't shake it.

One day shortly after Mama and Kathy had been gone, Daddy went to the hospital, and when he came home that evening, his face was red and swollen and I could tell he had been crying. He pulled Paul and Tommy aside to talk to them, and without saying a word to me, he changed into his work clothes and left the house. Something was wrong, but I didn't dare ask what.

The next morning, Daddy told us to take baths and get clean clothes on. We were going to the hospital to see Kathy. I was so happy. It had been so long since she and Mama had left. I imagined and wanted so much to believe that she must be all better and we were going there to bring her and Mama home.

When we got to the hospital, Tommy and I weren't allowed to go up to her room because we were under twelve years of age. I was upset that Paul got to go, but it was okay because I knew that any minute the elevator doors would open and Kathy would be standing there. Tommy and I sat downstairs for what seemed to be hours. Finally we took charge of two wheelchairs waiting by the door to transport patients in and out of the hospital. We raced up and down the hallway, and for the first time in such a long time, I had fun. I felt completely happy. Life was going to be normal again. Daddy and Paul never came back downstairs. Neither did Mama and Kathy. Time and time again, I watched the elevator doors open and close again, but Kathy was never on it. Later on in the day, two of Mama's sisters, Aunt Eleanor and Aunt Pauline, came to the hospital. Aunt Pauline took Tommy with her and they went back to the farm. I was told to go with Aunt Eleanor, who lived there in Nashville. We weren't given a reason why we had to go or where everybody was. We were just told to go. During the drive there and all day, Aunt Eleanor never spoke to me. We stayed at her house all day and until late in the afternoon when she received a telephone call telling her to bring me home.

On the drive back to the farm, she finally spoke to me. She glanced over at me and said, "Your sister has gone to live with the angels." That's all she said. She gave no explanation. Death, dying, heaven, and angels was something that was never discussed at our house, and I think now of how unbelievable and naive that it sounds, but in my eight years of life, no one I knew had ever died, not even a pet, and being told that Kathy had gone "to live with the angels" scared me. I didn't understand where she had gone. I wanted to ask Aunt Eleanor what she meant, but the words just wouldn't come.

When we arrived home, Daddy, Paul, and Tommy were there, but Mama and Kathy were not. Once again Daddy changed into his work clothes and went back out in the fields without saying a word to anybody. Aunt Eleanor busied herself in the kitchen making supper while Paul and Tommy stayed in their bedroom with the door shut. Once again I was alone. The events of the day raced through my mind and I tried to make some sense of what was going on, but I couldn't. Rather than stay in the house with Aunt Eleanor, I went outside and hid where neither she nor anybody else could see me, and I cried.

It was bedtime before Daddy came in. I was already in the bed, but I could hear him talking to Aunt Eleanor, and although I couldn't hear what they were saying, I could tell that he was crying.

Another day came and went, and that afternoon, when Daddy came in from work, he told us to put on our Sunday clothes. The four of us drove into town. We went to a building I had seen before but had never been to. Before we ever went in the door, Daddy and Paul started tearing up.

There were so many cars and, inside, so many people. When we walked through the doors, everyone stopped talking and turned to stare at us. Without saying anything to me, Daddy reached down and picked me up in his arms and we walked down the aisle toward a beautiful pink bed. When I looked down, there she was. It was Kathy. She was dressed in the white dress and veil that she wore for her first communion. She looked so beautiful. I thought she was asleep even though something bothered me about the way she looked. She was too still, and it was as though she wasn't real.

It had been weeks since I had seen her, and all I wanted to do was touch her and wake her up, but when I reached down to touch her cheek, Daddy grabbed my hand and said, "Don't touch her. You'll wake her up. She's asleep now. Kathy's not sick anymore." I hugged Daddy's neck as tight as I could even though I knew he wouldn't want me to.

Every time I recall this day, and even now when I write about it, I'm still amazed that I actually thought Kathy was alive, asleep, and well again. I have to remember, too, that I was just eight years old. No one had prepared me for or warned me about what I was going to see—just the opposite. They had done nothing but give me hope. Something wasn't right and I knew it, but I believed them. What else could I do?

We turned and walked out of the building without speaking to anyone, and I could see that everyone was crying and I didn't understand why. How could they be sad when it was such a happy day? That afternoon, the house started filling up with people. They brought tons of food and put it in the kitchen, and I actually thought we were having a party for Kathy.

After we ate, the children were told to go outside and play, and that's when I caught a glimpse of Mama going in the back door. I hadn't seen her all that day, not even when we went to see Kathy, but finally she was home, and I couldn't wait to see her.

I ran up the front porch and pushed the front door open, and when I did, I heard something crash to the floor. I looked down to see a small concrete angel lying on the floor. I had knocked it over, and one of its arms broke off. Everything got so silent, and the next thing I heard was Daddy screaming, "Look what you've done. You've broken the last thing that I can ever give Kathy. Get out of here. Get out and stay out." He was crying and he was screaming and everyone was looking at me. I stood paralyzed. I looked at him and then at the angel with her arm broken off and back at him again, and again he screamed, "Get out of here." I turned and ran out the door, slamming it behind me.

At the side of the house, there was a big, old oak tree. There was huge hole in the trunk that had been hollowed out with time. It was just big enough for me to fit into. It was there that I went to hide whenever I was scared or felt alone. It was the only place I could hide where no one would see me. I drew up into a ball, and a thousand questions ran through my mind. Why was Daddy crying? What was the angel for? Why was it the last thing he could give her? I thought about the pink bed. Why did it have a lid? I had never understood why everyone was so sad, even Paul and Tommy. Why weren't they happy? Was Kathy really coming home?

It was at that moment and that thought that I realized it: Kathy wasn't coming home. Not today, not ever. I didn't know where she had gone, but I knew that she was never coming back home. To describe what I felt at that moment is impossible.

I stayed outside by myself the rest of the day and hid. I peered around the tree and watched as people came and went, and even after the last person left, I didn't venture back inside the house. Daddy had never screamed at me before, and he had done it in front of so many people. Finally I heard Mama calling my name. I ran to the corner of the house and I could see her. She was carrying a suitcase. I grabbed onto her waist and she hugged me for only a second, just long enough to kiss me and tell me goodbye. She was going home with Aunt Pauline to New York City. She needed some time away. That's all she told me. As she walked to the car, I grabbed onto her skirt and pulled at her. I begged her not to go, but she didn't answer me. She couldn't. She was crying too hard. I held on to her as long as I could before Paul finally pulled me away from her and I watched as she drove away.

Kathy was diagnosed with cancer in April. She died in August. My world was turned upside down.

In September, one month later, Mama came back home just in time for school to start. She looked rested and had stopped crying, although she stayed sad all the time and hardly talked. I just wanted her to grab me up and hug me and love me like she had Kathy, but she rarely talked and never smiled. She went through her everyday routine, cooking and cleaning and doing what she had to do around the house. She seemed to be in a world all her own. So did Daddy.

It wasn't long before the sadness that had overtaken Mama and Daddy turned into bitterness. They screamed and fought all the time. They fought because we didn't have any money, they fought about the doctor bills they couldn't pay, and they fought because Mama went away for so long and left Daddy to run the farm and take care of us. They each blamed each other for their lives being so out of control. I don't remember there ever being many happy times in our home, but when Kathy died, it pretty much destroyed anything that was there. Whatever Mama and Daddy may have felt for each other was gone, and our lives—Paul's and Tommy's and mine—didn't matter, not to them. We sat aside, we watched, and we listened and waited for whatever was to happen next. I often wonder what our lives might have been like had Kathy not died, but it's hard to imagine. It stayed in the back of my mind that if I had gone away instead of Kathy, then everything would be the same again. Mama and Daddy would be happy again. Everyone would be.

One day, Mama told me she was taking me to see Kathy. Not a day had gone by since her death that I hadn't hoped for this day, and although I had come to the realization that she was never coming home, it was still in the back of my mind and I needed to believe that maybe someday she might.

We drove into town and then down the back streets that led to the cemetery. I had never been there or seen it, and I was amazed at all the concrete statues and wondered what they were for. We turned down one of the pathways, Mama stopped the car, and we walked in and out of the statues before she stopped and pointed to the ground. Very simply, she said, "Molly, Kathy's here." I looked down at the mound of dirt and then back at Mama and I didn't understand. What was she saying? Where was Kathy? When I glanced back at the grave, that's when I saw it. There it was. The tiny concrete angel with its arm broken off, and in front of it was a tiny square piece of concrete that read "Kathy Williams. Born January 20, 1955. Died August 15, 1959."

I can't explain what happened to me at that moment. I looked from Mama to the mound of dirt and back at her, and I remember screaming "Where, Mama? Where is she?"

I watched as Mama pointed to the ground and said, "She's buried here, Molly. Kathy's in heaven now. She's not sick anymore."

I remember just staring at the ground, trying to make some sense of what she was telling me. Suddenly all the events that had happened since Kathy first got sick and everything that was said to me started racing through my mind. "Kathy's getting better. Soon she'll be coming home." They had lied. Everyone had lied to me. Kathy was never coming home. She was there buried in the ground in that pink bed with the lid on it.

I dropped to the ground and started screaming at Mama, "She can't breathe, Mama. She can't breathe." I started pulling at the grass, screaming, "Help me, Mama. Help me get her out." I didn't realize what I was doing until I felt Mama pulling at me and screaming at me to stop. I was trying my best to dig Kathy out of the ground. What happened after that and the rest of that day, I don't remember at all, but the nightmares started and wouldn't stop. Even during the day, all I could think of and see inside my head was Kathy buried in the ground in her white dress and veil and the lid of that pink bed closed up tight on top of her and Kathy couldn't breathe and I needed to get her out. I couldn't eat, I couldn't sleep, and at times I felt like I couldn't breathe. I cried all the time, but always in private where no one could see me. I knew better than to talk about it. I knew better than to ask questions. I had no one to help me figure out what had happened. If Mama told anyone about that day, it was never mentioned, not ever.

All these years later, out of all the things I remember and have written about, this is the one that still brings tears to my eyes. This is the one memory that totally breaks me down.

Kathy had died in August. Mama and Daddy divorced that December. Her death was just too much for them. For some reason, they blamed each other. It not only destroyed my parents, but I wonder if they ever realized what it did to me and my brothers.

Shortly thereafter, Mama, my brothers, and I moved away from the farm to a neighboring town. I remember the day that we left. Daddy stood by the car crying, begging Mama not to take us away. As we pulled away from the house, I looked out the back window at him. He was standing in the middle of the road, dirt flying in his face. I waved at him, but he didn't wave back. The thought ran through my mind again. If only it had been me. Nothing would have changed. Kathy was everything to everybody. I wasn't. Why couldn't it have been me?

I don't think a day has gone by since Kathy's death that I haven't thought about it. I have to assume that Mama and Daddy thought they were protecting me by not telling me the truth, or maybe they thought I was too young and wouldn't understand, or just maybe it didn't seem to matter to them how it affected me. Whatever the reason, things needed to be explained. It might not have had such a long-term effect on me.

Once upon a time, I had a family, whole and complete. My parents weren't happy together, but at least we were together. They say that when parents aren't happy, it's probably better for the children if they divorce. For Mama and Daddy, it probably was for the best—but not for me and not for my brothers.

As far as I know, Mama never went back to the cemetery. If she did, she went alone. Very rarely have I gone either. It's just too hard. When I stand over her grave, I can still see her tiny body, dressed in the white dress and veil, and as hard as I try, I can't get the vision out of my head. All that's left of Kathy is the tiny concrete angel with only one arm lifted to heaven.

Just recently, I replaced the angel. I replaced it with a beautiful angel that stands four feet tall. She has a band of flowers circling her head and she has two arms reaching for heaven. I called Daddy to tell him what I had done. There was complete silence on the other end of the line. Finally, in a strained voice, he said, "Don't throw her angel away."

I told him I didn't intend to throw it away. I thought replacing the angel would finally make things right between us, and not only with him, but with Kathy too. After all, it was the last thing he could give her.

The new home we moved to was extremely small. I had to share a bedroom with Mama. Almost every night for I don't know how long, maybe years, Mama would wake me up in the middle of the night saying, "Molly, wake up. Kathy's here. Do you see her?" She always pointed to the end of the bed. "She's there, Molly. Do you see her? She wants me to come with her."

Of course I never saw Kathy, but I did believe she was there, and it was important to Mama that I see Kathy. So I would sit straight up in the bed and always tell Mama, "Yes, I see her." I would listen while Mama talked to her. It was as though they were carrying on a real conversation, and I wished so hard that I could see Kathy too. At the end of their conversation, Mama would always tell Kathy, "I love you. I can't come right now, but I'll be there soon. Wait for me." Then Mama would lie back down in the bed and cry herself to sleep.

Mama wanted to die. I knew she wanted to be with Kathy, but I didn't want her to go, and so when I lay back down in the bed, I would whisper to Kathy, "Please go away. Please leave Mama alone. I want her to stay with me," and then I would cry myself to sleep too.

Kathy was alone. She was out there somewhere, and she was alone. She needed Mama, but I needed her more. The thought of Mama dying was more than I could imagine, and as much as I loved Kathy, I wanted her to go away and leave Mama alone. It was just more guilt to pack onto what was already more than I could carry.

SISTER ANNE

Kathy had died in August. Mama and Daddy divorced in December. Immediately after they went to court to finalize everything, Mama came home and packed up and we moved to a neighboring town twenty minutes away from the farm. We left the only home I had ever known, and we left my grandparents who had been a major part of my life. Little did I know that it would be six long years before I would see them again. Mama wouldn't allow it. According to her, Mammie was one of the main causes of the divorce. I'll agree that Mammie was outspoken and she did give her opinion, even when it wasn't asked for, but she wasn't the cause of the divorce. There were so many other factors, the main one being Kathy's death.

Half of the school year was over, and for what was left, my brothers and I were enrolled in a private parochial school, St. John Vianney Catholic School. There were only three classrooms in the school and three nuns to teach them. Children were divided up into three rooms—first, second, and third; fourth and fifth; and sixth, seventh, and eighth—and in each classroom were fifteen to twenty students. The teachers were Dominican nuns, and because of their dress, I thought they were enchanting and also mysterious. They wore long black gowns that hung to the floor, and around their waists hung long rosary beads with a cross at the end. They wore black-and-white veils around their heads, which covered everything up but their faces. The only other visible parts of their bodies were their hands. Everything else was covered completely.

I was in the last half of the third grade, and my teacher was Sister Marie Therese, who was probably in her early twenties. She had a beautiful porcelain-white face and dark black eyebrows.

Mama had told me that the nuns shaved their heads, but it was impossible to believe that Sister Marie Therese had no hair. She was exceptionally kind to all of the children in the class, but she seemed to show me extra attention. I figure she must have been told about Kathy's death and my parents' divorce. Every day, I looked forward to getting to school just so I could be with her, and I started to believe that everything worked out for the best. Little did I know what was ahead for me.

Summer came and school ended and I had finally settled into my new home and made friends with the neighborhood children. I still missed Mammie and Papa, and I missed Daddy too. I had not seen or heard from him since we moved away. Every day I hoped he would come see, us but he never did.

When school started back in the fall, I moved to the fourth-and-fifth-grade room. Sister Anne was my teacher. It was her first year at St. John's, and although she was much older than Sister Marie Therese, I was hopeful that she would be as kind. She wasn't. She was just the opposite. She was a short, extremely obese woman who looked to be in her fifties, and because of her weight, she walked with the aid of a cane. It was hard for her to walk, so all day long she sat behind her desk. Her teaching consisted of screaming and pounding the cane on the floor, and I wondered many times why she had chosen to be a nun. It was obvious that she hated what she did.

Mama had once told me that the nuns were brides of Christ. They wore a small, gold wedding band on their left hand to prove that. Mama believed that whatever they said or did was the right thing and was not to be questioned. It was hard to imagine that Sister Anne was a bride of Christ. Just being in her presence horrified me. Very early on, my intuition told me that my experience in her room would be bad. I just didn't know how bad.

Every morning, first thing, we were marched next door to the church for Mass. One nun led us to the church and another nun followed behind to make sure there was no talking or misbehavior. Once the Mass started, we had to either stand or kneel. There was no sermon and therefore no reason to sit, and if for any reason one of us attempted to sit down, one of the nuns confronted you, made you hold your hand out, and spanked your palm with her ruler. There were mornings when I hadn't had time to eat breakfast before school, as I'm sure many students didn't. I would feel weak and the need to sit down, but I didn't dare, seeing what happened to those who did. I came to fear the nuns. They weren't there just to teach us. They were there to rule us and punish us, and I began to feel like my days were spent in prison.

Along with the other subjects taught to us, we were also taught catechism—religion. The only thing I remember the nuns teaching me about God was that he was to be feared. Everything about him was negative. I don't remember ever being taught that he was a loving God who would help me if I prayed to him. From the time I could remember, Mama had always insisted that I get down on my knees every night at bedtime and say my prayers, and it had always comforted me. But my time under the nuns changed my feelings about God. The only possible sins I ever committed was fighting with Tommy or sassing Mama. Every week, I had to profess my sins to God through the priest, and every week my sins were the same and I prayed for forgiveness. If I didn't pray for forgiveness and receive it then I would surely go to hell. I wanted to profess the sin I had committed with Uncle Tea to the priest, but I didn't dare. So every night at bedtime I said my own prayers to God and professed the sin directly to him. I asked for forgiveness but was convinced that he either wasn't listening or was not going to forgive me. The Catholic school and the nuns were my punishment.

Midway through the year, we had started learning our times tables. I enjoyed math, and it seemed to be the only subject I was really good in. Every night, Mama listened to me recite them over and over again until there was no hesitation, until I said them perfectly. I was so proud of myself that I couldn't wait until the next day to recite them. Sister Anne was always pleased with the students when they were able to say them without faltering, and for some reason, I wanted her to be proud of me.

There were eight or nine students in the fourth grade that year including myself. When it came time to recite our times table, we were told to line up in front of the blackboard. We were used to Sister Anne screaming and pounding her cane on the floor when one of us couldn't say them perfectly, but that's all she ever did. As furious as she got, she had never gotten physical with any child. One day, when it came my turn to recite, I managed to get through the ones through fours, but midway through the fives, I couldn't finish. I could not say five times five. It was a complete blank, and as hard as I tried to get it out, it just wasn't there. Sister Anne had already screamed at several of the children before me who weren't able to complete their tables, and although I was confident that I could say mine, her screaming shook me up and fear took me over. My throat tightened up and I shook all over. Sister Anne had never screamed at me, but I had never given her a reason to.

When I couldn't finish saying my five times table, she pounded her cane on the floor and screamed at me "Molly, did you study?"

All I could get out was, "Yes, Sister."

"Then why don't you know them?" she screamed. "Start over."

And so I did, but when I got to five times five, again I couldn't finish them.

She told the girl standing next to me to start reciting, and without taking a breath, she screamed at me again, "Molly, when I come back around, you'd better be ready."

When I didn't look up at her, again she screamed, "Molly, look at me. Did you hear me?"

Like a tiny mouse, I barely uttered the words "Yes, Sister."

The girl standing next to me recited her fives perfectly and the next child and the next child, all the way down the line and back around, and then it was my turn again.

Still shaking, I stood frozen and my throat locked up.

"Molly," she screamed, "recite your fives." I didn't look at her, and I couldn't speak.

Again, "Molly, recite your fives."

That's when she screamed, "Come up here."

Reluctantly, with my legs shaking so hard that I could hardly walk, I made my way to her desk and stood in front of her. All I could think of was, "Oh God, what's she going to do?"

Because I didn't get close enough to her, she yelled, "Get over here!"

When I did, she reached out and slapped my across the face so hard that I fell to the floor. I lay there stunned, and for a second I didn't realize what had happened, not until I heard her scream, "Get up."

When I stood up, I sensed a warming between my legs, and looking down, I realized that I had peed on myself.

"Look what you've done. You've made a mess," she said. "Go to the bathroom, get paper towels, and come back in here and clean it up."

I was in such shock that I couldn't move. I looked from her to the floor and back at her, and that's when she screamed her orders again. It was almost as though I was in a trance. I turned and walked to the door, opened it, and walked out into the hall where I saw Sister Marie Therese and the principal, Sister Mary Albert, standing. I looked away from them down at the floor, and as I walked past them, Sister Mary Albert stopped me, put her hand on my chin, and raised my face to look at her. That's when the tears started flowing. Without saying a word, she motioned me to go on to the bathroom and retrieve the towels.

The bathroom was right next to the back door that led to the playground. For one brief second, I stood there with my hand on the doorknob and wondered, "If I run, who's fast enough to catch me?" But then it ran through my mind, "If I run and they do catch me, what will she do to me then?"

I had no choice. I turned and walked into the bathroom, pulled out paper towels, wet them, and walked back to the classroom. Both nuns were still standing there watching me, still and quiet. When I opened the door and walked back into the classroom, there wasn't a sound to be heard. The children sat quietly, and all eyes were on me. I got down on my knees and wiped the urine up and then stood in front of Sister Anne waiting for her next command.

I was crying so hard that I could hardly mutter the words, but finally I managed to say, "Can I call my Mama to come get me?"

She didn't hesitate with her answer. "You're not calling anybody," she screamed. "Get in that chair and sit down."

"Please, Sister," I said, "I want my Mama."

"Sit down and be quiet," she screamed.

She motioned to the desk sitting next to her, the desk we were told to sit in if she punished us. It was turned away from the rest of the class and faced the wall. I took my seat, and there I sat the rest of the morning in sopping wet, urine-soaked clothes. I cried so hard that I made awful choking sounds and I couldn't stop, and because I couldn't stop crying, she made me lay my head down on the desk and threatened more punishment if I didn't stop.

"Maybe tonight you'll do your homework!" she screamed.

I didn't raise my head again, not until she released the rest of the class to go out on the playground. Even then I didn't budge, not until Nancy, my best friend, came and took me by the hand.

The other children had not ventured out onto the playground as they normally did. They stood at the bottom of the stairs waiting for me, and as I walked down toward them, they bombarded me with questions: "Did it hurt, Molly?" And one of the boys asked, "Why didn't you hit her back?"

I never answered them. I walked to the corner of the building, sat down, and pulled my knees to my head. There I buried my face and cried while they all stood and watched. Nancy sat with me. She cried too.

I kept going over and over in my mind what had happened and why she had gotten so mad at me. Sure, she had screamed and pounded her cane on the floor at almost every child in the classroom at some point, but she had never gotten physical or hurt any of them. So why me?

Mama was still at work when I got home from school that afternoon. I would only have thirty minutes before she arrived home. Hurriedly, I took my clothes off and put them in the washing machine, using only the rinse cycle. To wash them would have taken too long. When they were rinsed, I stuck them into the dryer; when they were dry, I put them back on. Mama would know something was wrong if I had fresh clothes on, and it wouldn't matter that she knew how hard I had studied the night before. The nuns could do no wrong. I would surely be punished for upsetting Sister Anne. Rarely did Mama get upset with me about anything, but I was positive that for this, I would be spanked. Whatever she did to me, it could never be as bad as what Sister Anne did. When Mama came in from work, I made every effort to avoid looking at her and acted as though nothing had happened. She didn't even notice how swollen my eyes were from crying.

All night long, I worried that the phone would ring and some parent would call to tell Mama what happened, but I also halfway hoped it would ring. It didn't matter what I hoped for. Nobody called. Not one parent called to check on me. I had to assume that, if they were told what happened, then they too felt like I deserved it.

I stayed in my room studying that night until I could no longer hold my eyes opened. I was determined that I'd never give Sister Anne another reason to hurt me, but it was no use. The very next day, we were told to take our places at the blackboard and again recite our times table. The first go-around, I didn't falter, although I could hardly get the words out. When it came back around to me the second time, I couldn't speak.

Sister Anne screamed, "Molly, did you study last night?"

I started feeling sick and weak and thought I was going to fall down.

"Molly, look at me," she screamed again. "Did you study last night?"

I wanted to tell her that I was sick, but there was no time. Vomit rolled out my mouth onto my book, onto the floor, and onto the two empty desks in front of me.

Mama had cooked a roast, potatoes, carrots, and peas the night before. I had not been hungry. My nerves were shot, but Mama insisted that I clean my plate.

"You're lucky to have this food," she said, so I choked it down.

When I vomited, that's exactly what came out—in chunks—meat, potatoes, carrots, and peas. The kids standing next to me scattered away from me as fast as they could.

When the vomiting ceased, Sister Anne started screaming at me again, "Look what you've done! You've made a mess."

It was all I could do to tell her, "I'm sorry, Sister. I'm sick."

"You did this on purpose," she screamed. "You're not sick. You didn't study last night, did you?"

I cried and pleaded with her, "Yes, Sister, I did study, but I'm sick."

"Stop lying," she screamed.

I waited for the order to come to her desk so she could slap me, but to my surprise, she didn't.

Instead she screamed, "Go to the bathroom and get what you need to clean up this mess up, and hurry up!"

"Yes, Sister," I said. I walked past the other children, and as I started to exit the room, I reached out to throw my book in the trash can.

"Don't you throw that book away," she said.

I held the book up for her to see and said, "It's ruined, Sister."

"Be quiet," she said. "You're going to use that book the rest of the year, and every time you open it, it will be a reminder that you had better study before you come back into my classroom."

At that moment, in a defiant manner, and I still can't believe I did it, I slammed the book shut as hard as I could. Peas, potatoes, carrots, and meat squeezed out of the pages. It took only one second for me to realize what I had done, and panic rushed over me. She'd surely get me now. I stood still, not looking at her. I stared at the floor and I waited. I waited for the demand to come to her desk, and I prepared myself. It would hurt, but I was determined that I would not fall down and I would not pee on myself, not again. I don't know what came over me. As sick as I was and as scared as I was, I was determined that I would stand strong. I would take whatever came next. Slowly, I looked up at Sister Anne, who sat still in her chair and stared at me.

She didn't scream this time but said in a calm voice, "Clean that mess up."

I walked back over to my desk and laid my book down and then walked out into the hallway and to the bathroom. I retrieved paper towels and returned to the room. I got down on my knees and cleaned the floor and the desks that were drenched in vomit. There was not a sound to be heard in the classroom, not a whisper, not a movement.

When I was finished, I calmly asked Sister Anne if I could call Mama to come get me, knowing all well what the answer would be.

"You are not calling your mother to come get you," she said.

"But my clothes, Sister."

"Sit down and be quiet," she said. "You're going to keep those clothes on all day, and maybe tonight you'll study." I took my place in the desk next to her and faced the wall, and as hard as I tried, I couldn't hold the tears back. But I turned my head away from her. No matter what, I would not let her see me cry.

That afternoon when I got home from school, I changed out of my filthy clothes, and as the day before, I put them in the washer, dried them, and put them back on. Mama never sensed that anything was wrong, and I never told her what happened, not any of it. All night long, again, I waited for the phone to ring. This time, I prayed that someone would call and tell her and that my days at St. John's would be over with. I was certain of it. I'd never have to go back. I waited and I waited, but the phone never rang. That night, when I got down on my knees to say my prayers, I didn't pray. Instead I asked God, "Why don't you like me?" Mama had told me for as long as I could remember, "If you're a good little girl, God will always protect you." So where was he?

Sister Anne never disciplined me again that year, but then I gave her no reason to. I had always studied hard and strived to make good grades, but after that experience, I was harder on myself than anybody else could be. I was never satisfied with anything but an A. Maybe that was the only good thing that came out of it.

Sister Anne didn't come back to St. John's the next year or any year after that.

Six years later, when I was a sophomore in high school, Nancy came up to me one day, all excited. "Molly, my mother told me to tell you Sister Anne died. She sat down in a chair and it collapsed. She broke her hip and was forced to stay in the bed. She died shortly after of pneumonia. Mama wanted you to know. I was so happy when I heard it. I hope it makes you happy too," and then she hugged me.

"Thank you, Nancy," was all I could say. As I walked away from her, tears rolled down my cheeks. Rather than happiness, I was consumed with sadness and with guilt. I had prayed time after time that Sister Anne would die for what she did to me. I had prayed that she'd burn in hell, and at that moment, God ran through my mind. Maybe he was listening to my prayers after all.

Sam was one of the boys in my fourth grade classroom that year. At my high school ten-year class reunion, he spotted me and came over with his wife. He introduced me to her, saying, "This is the girl I told you about." He related the story to her about Sister Anne slapping me and the day I vomited all over everything.

He continued to say, "I hated so bad that she hurt you, Molly. It has affected me my whole life, and I wouldn't doubt that it affected every kid in that classroom who witnessed it. My two children go to a

Catholic school," he went on to say, "and their teachers are Dominican nuns. Before they ever started to school, I told them about you and what happened. I made them promise that if anyone, even the nuns, ever hurt them they should tell me and I would help them. After that happened to you, I promised myself that no matter what, I would protect my children from everyone and everything, and every day of their lives, I remind them that I am there to protect them. Sister Anne should have been locked away for what she did to you."

When he finished, I asked him, "Why didn't you tell your parents, Sam?"

I wasn't shocked when he said, "I did."

"No one ever called my mother to tell her, and I prayed that someone would."

"You know how it was Molly," he said. "The nuns could do no wrong, and no one wanted to get involved."

And there it was. How many people knew what Sister Anne had done to me? Even the other nuns in the school knew it, and still they protected her. But you know what? Maybe she was punished after all. Maybe her punishment was not being sent back to St. John's to teach. Maybe she was never allowed to teach again. If that's all that happened to her, though, it wasn't enough. If she hurt a child like that today, she would probably be put in prison. Now all I have is knowing that she is dead and can't hurt anyone ever again.

Every time I finish writing one of my journals, I think back about myself and the kind of child I was then. In my short ten years of life, a lot had happened; too much had happened. I was a quiet, sweet, shy little girl, but I was always overwhelmed with sadness, and added to that was constant fear. I never felt safe. Every day of my life, I woke up with the dread of what that day would bring and who would be there to protect me.

THE MILKMAN

After Mama and Daddy divorced and we moved away, we settled into our new house. I called it the Cracker Jack box. It was no bigger than seven hundred square feet and was the smallest house I had ever been in. Although we lived in a neighborhood where there were lots of kids to play with, I hated it. It would never be my home. My home would always be the farm.

There were only two bedrooms, so I had to share my bedroom with Mama. She smoked in the bed at night, and the smoke consumed our room. It was so hard to breathe, but I knew better than to complain. Mama slept on the outside and I had to sleep against the wall. I wasn't allowed to turn over or move during the night because it would wake Mama up; as hard as I tried, I couldn't be still. Every night, Uncle Tea came back into my dreams to haunt me, and every night, Mama would shake me and tell me to stop screaming. Not once did she ask me why I was screaming or what the nightmare was about.

I did not see or hear from Daddy after we moved away. I knew that he called Mama on the telephone from time to time, and I would sit by quietly and listen and hope so much that he would ask to talk to me, but he never did. Although I missed him, all I could remember about Daddy was the anger in his voice and the hate in his eyes that day of Kathy's funeral. I had not been able to look him in the face after that day, and he never looked at me either. The day we moved away, he had not even said goodbye.

One day, almost a year after we had moved, there was a knock on the front door. When I opened it, there Daddy stood. I looked up at him for only an instant before looking down at the ground.

The shame of what I had done came rushing back over me and I had to choke back the tears. He didn't try to hug me or kiss me but simply said, "Is your Mama here?" It was as though I was a stranger.

As soon as Mama came to the door, I disappeared into my bedroom and shut the door behind me. I waited for them to start arguing and screaming, but they didn't. In fact, I could hardly hear them at all. I didn't venture out of my room until I heard Daddy leave. Mama never told us what he wanted, but after that day she seemed happy for a change. Daddy started calling and coming around a lot, and he and Mama started going out on dates and spending time together. It had been so long since I had seen Mama smile, and so I was glad Daddy was back.

Time passed away and life felt like it was coming back together. Mama was happy and didn't seem so stressed out all the time. Daddy was around more, but still he seemed so far away. He had a good relationship with Paul and Tommy, but for me there seemed to be nothing there. It only confirmed what I had always known. He wished I had died instead of Kathy.

Mama and Daddy were remarried in June of 1961. I was so excited, but not because Daddy would be living with us again. We would be moving back home, back to the farm, back to Mammie and Papa. Life would make sense again, and for the first time in a very long time, I felt happy and hopeful too.

It didn't take but a few seconds for Mama to burst that bubble. We weren't going home. We were moving across town to a nicer neighborhood and a bigger house. The disappointment in my face must have shown, because immediately Mama said, "Molly, you're gonna have your own bedroom." That in itself was something to be happy about.

We moved to the big house across town, and although I liked it, it was strange having Daddy live with us again. I had gotten used to life without him, and it felt almost as though we had a stranger living with us. He still made me feel as though I was invisible, but it didn't matter about me. I just wanted Mama to be happy.

Every night at bedtime, I got down on my knees and prayed to God, "I don't care where we live, God, just let Mama and Daddy be happy. Let us all be happy." Sometimes, I guess, prayers are answered. Mine never were. I was convinced that God didn't know I was alive. If he did, he didn't care. Not about me.

It wasn't long after we moved to the new house that Mama and Daddy started screaming at each other again. Daddy wanted to move back to the farm, but Mama refused, and so to try and keep peace, Daddy took a job in a tire factory. Monday through Friday he worked at the factory, and on the weekends he farmed. Rarely was he home except to sleep, but even then the screaming never stopped. At least when we lived on the farm, there were places to escape to so I wouldn't have to hear it, but there was no place to escape to in the city. The neighbors lived right on top of us, and there was nowhere to go but the backyard. I often wondered if my friends could hear the yelling and screaming. I would have hated that. I didn't want anyone to know how unhappy my family was.

Not long after we had moved to the new house, a milk company salesman stopped by to see Mama. His name was Mr. Thompson, and the name on the side of his truck was "Thompson's Milk Company." The company was, in fact, owned by his family. He was tall like Daddy, had dark hair like Daddy, and was handsome like Daddy, but unlike Daddy, he was nice and he smiled a lot. Mama placed an order with him to have bottled milk brought to our house, and he would even bring it inside and put in the refrigerator. Mama said it was a small luxury she deserved and it would save her some unnecessary trips to the grocery store.

Mr. Thompson seemed to be around the same age as Daddy, thirty-seven years old. I was only ten years old at the time. It amazes me still that neither Mama nor Daddy knew anything about this man, but yet they trusted him to come into our home twice a week to put milk into our refrigerator. I heard Mama tell him that first day he came to our house, "Molly will always be here to let you in." I couldn't believe it then and still can't believe it now. She never gave one thought to my safety.

Mama and Daddy were usually gone to work by 6:00 or 6:30

every morning. My brother, Paul, was sixteen and had a summer job downtown at a men's store. Tommy was twelve, and every morning he took just long enough to cram a bite of breakfast into his mouth before he took out on his bicycle to places unknown with his friends. I had two girlfriends who lived in the neighborhood, Cindy and Connie, but neither of them was allowed to come to my house because there was no adult supervision. Mama had given me the job of making all the beds, cleaning the kitchen, and picking up the house, and for that I was given a small allowance every week. After finishing the house work, I either watched television or played with my Barbie doll. For seven or eight hours every day, I was left alone in the house all by myself.

Mr. Thompson always delivered our milk on the same day of the week and around the same time, every Tuesday and Thursday morning at 10:00 AM, and rarely was he late. At first I shied away from him and hid in the back part of the house when he came in, but he knew I was there. He usually tapped on the door before coming in, and he always called for me, "Dolly, are you here?" That's what he called me from the very start, "Dolly" instead of Molly, because, he said, "I was as pretty as a doll." No one had ever given me a nickname, and I liked it. Mr. Thompson made me feel special, and I know now that he knew just what to do to gain my trust. After Uncle Tea molested me, I had never let any man touch me—not even to hug me. Not Daddy, and not Papa either. Of course, Daddy never tried. I learned very early on that men were not to be trusted, and I made my mind up that no matter how nice Mr. Thompson was to me, I would make sure he never got close enough to touch me.

It wasn't long after Mr. Thompson started coming to the house that I felt comfortable enough to come out of my bedroom to talk to him. His routine was the same every time he came. He put the milk in our refrigerator, wrote out the ticket for Mama, and then always stayed a few minutes longer to talk to me. Our conversations always centered around his children and me and my brothers. He had two sons and a daughter my same age. Every time he came, he had a new story to tell me about her, and he would show me the pictures he carried of her in his wallet. I could tell he loved her a lot, and I found myself feeling jealous. Daddy didn't carry any pictures of me; I was sure of that. I started looking forward to Mr. Thompson coming to the house the way I should have felt when I knew Daddy was coming home, but Daddy wasn't like him. He never spoke to me when he came home.

Mr. Thompson was always curious about Mama and Daddy and the whereabouts of my brothers. Once, not long after he had been delivering our milk, I remember him saying to me, "Dolly, you're always alone, aren't you?" and innocently, I said, "Yes." I never suspected a thing.

Mr. Thompson had been delivering milk to us well into the summer when something about him changed. He was always nice to me, but something about him made me feel a little afraid. There were times when he talked to me that it felt he was looking straight through me. I started shying away from him and staying in the back part of the house again. Every time he came, though, he still called out for me, "Dolly, I know you're there. Come out and talk to me."

One day Mr. Thompson came earlier than usual. I was in the kitchen doing the dishes and didn't hear him come in the back door. He had always knocked first, but that day he didn't. All of a sudden, when I turned around, he was standing there in the kitchen, just staring at me. When I took a deep breath and stepped back, he apologized for scaring me, but I couldn't answer him. My heart was pounding so hard that I couldn't speak, and it was as though I was frozen. I knew I needed to run to my room, but for some reason I couldn't move. He stepped around me to put the milk on the counter and started making small talk. He asked me how the summer was going and if I had been to the swimming pool, and then he turned around, looked at me, and said, "You're beautiful, Dolly. Do you know that?"

The look in his eyes was one I had seen before—the same eyes as Uncle Tea. That's when I turned to run, but he caught me and backed me up against the refrigerator. He pressed his body up against me and held my arms above me so I couldn't move. I started crying and begged him to let me go, but it was as though he didn't hear me. He grabbed my cheeks and forced me to look at him. He had to see the horror in my eyes. "Dolly, I love you," he said. "I'm not going to hurt you. Just be still." But he was going to hurt me and I knew it. It was happening all over again.

Mr. Thompson's face turned bright red and he was breathing hard just like Uncle Tea had. He held both of my arms above my head with one hand, and with his other hand he started stroking my hair. "You have such beautiful hair, Dolly," he said.

As hard as I tried and as much as I begged, I couldn't push him away. I wanted to scream but nothing would come out, and what good would it do? There was nobody anywhere around to help me.

He kept saying, "Shhh, Dolly. Don't be afraid. I'm not going to hurt you. I love you. You're just like my little girl."

All I could think about was what Uncle Tea had made me do to him. He made me perform oral sex on him. I couldn't imagine having to do that again. I cried and I screamed and, as hard as I could, I tried to push him away, but I was just too small to fight him. What scared me more than anything, I think, was how nervous he was and how much he was shaking. He seemed to be as afraid as I was.

That day, I had pink shorts on and a little pink-checked blouse that buttoned up the front with tiny white pearl buttons. Mama made the outfit for me herself by hand, and I was so proud of it. Holding my arms above my head with his one hand, he proceeded to put his other hand up my blouse and touched my breasts. My breasts had started growing slightly, just enough to wear a training bra. When he forced his hand up my blouse, one of the tiny pearl buttons popped off, and I heard it hit the floor. As scared as I was, at that second what went through my mind was how I would explain the button to Mama.

Mr. Thompson started kissing me all over my face, moving his mouth from my lips to my cheeks and then my neck. His breath was hot and his breathing heavy, and when I think back about it, it's as though he was kissing a grown woman, not a ten-year-old child. As I looked into his eyes with horror, I knew that this must be the face of the devil. It was beet red and wet with sweat.

Mr. Thompson proceeded to move his hand from my breasts down inside my shorts and then my panties, all the while holding my arms above my head. He touched my vagina and put his fingers up inside, and it hurt so bad, just as it had when Uncle Tea had done it. It felt like a knife cutting me up inside. As hard as I fought and pushed against him, I couldn't wrench myself free. He pressed his mouth against my cheeks and just kept saying, "Shhh, Dolly. I love you. I won't hurt you," and there was panic in his voice that scared me even more. I wished so hard that Mama or one of my brothers would come home and catch Mr. Thompson, but I knew they wouldn't and so did he.

Finally Mr. Thompson pulled his hands out of my panties, and with both hands he held my shoulders against the refrigerator. With his face pressed against mine, he said, "Calm down, Dolly. You're okay. I didn't hurt you." For one split second, he let go of me and started fooling with his pants. I guess he thought I wouldn't run, but I did. I pushed him away from me, and as fast as I could, I ran into my brothers' room, which was just off the kitchen, and I shut the door. Before I could lock it, he came through the door and pushed me down on the bed. Again I fought him with all I had, but he got into my face again and smothered me with his mouth. Just when I thought it was over, it was really just beginning.

Holding me down with one hand, he started working at unzipping his pants with his other hand. He had me pinned down with both arms above my head, and there was no way to get out from under him. I remember that all at once a peace came over me—a kind of calming. I became really still and stopped fighting him. What good would it do? This was going to happen and there was nothing I could do to stop it, and somehow I knew that if I didn't fight him, maybe he wouldn't hurt me. He must have realized it too, because he let go of me, and silently I just lay there.

"Be still, Dolly," he said. "Just be still a minute."

He stood up and started working with the buckle of his pants. I knew it might be the last chance I had to get away from him, so I drew my legs back to my waist. He wasn't paying any attention to me and didn't know it was coming when I kicked him. It caught him off guard and he fell backward onto the other twin bed. When he did, I flew off the bed and ran down the hall and into my room. I could hear him running after me, but I managed to get inside my room and locked the door behind me. I backed away from the door and stood there waiting for him to come through it. He jiggled the door handle and kept jiggling the doorknob and kept knocking, but I didn't answer.

After a few seconds, he got real angry and screamed again, "Open this door. I won't hurt you." Still I didn't answer. Instead I looked around the room to see where I could hide. There wasn't any place. I knew he would find me if I hid in the closet. The only other place was under the bed. I got down on my knees and looked under the bed. As low as it was to the floor, I was sure I could fit under it. I scooted to the middle as far as I could and up against the wall, hoping he wouldn't be able to reach me. I knew that at any second he would come through the door and I waited. To muffle the sounds of crying, I stuck my thumb in my mouth and sucked it. I drew my knees to my chest until I was in a fetal position and I watched under the door. I told myself, *"If I'm quiet as a mouse, he won't know I'm here."* I never took my eyes off of the door, and he didn't move. He stayed there for the longest time, knocking on the door and talking to me.

"Dolly," he said, "let me in. I'm sorry if I scared you. I promise I won't hurt you. Come out."

I don't know how long he stood there trying to talk me out, but it seemed like forever. Still sucking my thumb and drawn up in a knot, I closed my eyes and started thinking to myself, "What had I done to cause this? I had been nice to him. I had trusted him, and I promised myself from the start that I wouldn't. This was all my fault."

It's impossible to describe the fear I felt as I lay there under my bed watching his feet and listening to him. I didn't know what else to do but to pray. God had never answered my prayers before, but maybe if I prayed really hard, he would help me this time. And so I started praying.

Finally Mr. Thompson stopped talking and walked away from the door. I watched as he walked down the hall and into the kitchen. He's leaving, I thought. Then just as quickly as he walked away, he was back at my door trying to get in.

"Don't tell anybody what happened, Dolly," he said. "I don't want to hurt you. You have to keep our secret. Do you hear me? Don't you tell anyone."

I closed my eyes and pressed my hands over my ears, trying so hard not to listen to him. "Please go away," I cried silently. "Please go away." Then I watched as he walked away, down the hall, through the kitchen, and I heard the back door close.

I didn't come out from under my bed. I knew he might be tricking me. Instead I stayed drawn up in a fetal position and sucked my thumb. I shut my eyes and kept repeating to myself, *"If I'm quiet as a mouse, he won't know I'm here. If I'm quiet as a mouse, he won't know I'm here."*

Mr. Thompson always parked in the Henderson's driveway next door. My bedroom window was beside that driveway. I listened ever so quietly as I heard him get in his truck and slide the door closed. Then he started the truck up and backed out of the driveway, and I heard him drive away from the house. Still I didn't budge.

I lay under my bed for a long time after I heard his truck pull away. I shivered all over and couldn't stop crying, but I cried inside myself, just as I always had, so he wouldn't hear me if he had snuck back into the house. My body started cramping from being drawn up in a knot for so long and I hurt all over, but still I never moved an inch. I was afraid that he had moved his truck from the neighbor's house and pulled it around to the other side of my house. He knew I wouldn't hear him from there.

I don't know how long I continued to lie there listening for him before I finally decided to slide out from under the bed. I tiptoed to the window and peeked out the corner to make sure his truck wasn't there. It wasn't. I tiptoed across the room to my door and listened but could hear nothing. I got down on the floor and looked under the door to see if he was standing there. He wasn't. I was so scared to open that door. Putting my hand on that doorknob and opening that door was probably the most frightening thing I had ever had to do.

I opened it only a fraction so I could see into the hallway, prepared to shut it and lock it as fast as I could if he were to spring out at me. Finally I crept into the hall, stopped, and listened. There were no sounds to be heard. It was completely quiet. I started tiptoeing from room to room, stopping at each doorway before I entered. If he were to jump out from behind the door or the furniture, I wanted to give myself plenty of time to run. I looked out every window and behind every piece of furniture before leaving each room. Finally, after checking the other two bedrooms, the bathroom, and the living room, I stepped into the kitchen.

If he was in the house, he had to be in either the kitchen or the den. I stood still, listened, watched, and waited, prepared to make a dead run if I heard the slightest sound. Peering around the doorway, I could see that he wasn't in the kitchen. If indeed he did come back into the house, then the den was where he was. I stood frozen. Finally I took a deep breath and crept into the doorway of the den. Looking all around the room, I couldn't see him. Without giving it another thought, I ran as fast as I could to the back door and locked it. I ran over to the den window and looked out into the driveway. His truck wasn't there. He was gone.

Before I could take another breath, I felt it coming. I barely made it to the bathroom and to the commode before vomit started rolling out of my mouth. When no more would come, I laid my head on the side of the commode and once again cried my eyes out, but this time I didn't try to muffle the sounds. I cried out loud.

I must have passed out with my head on the commode for a short time. When I woke up, strands of my hair had fallen into the commode and were drenched with vomit. I raised myself up and walked to the sink. I washed the vomit out of my hair and out of my blouse and cleaned the sink and also the commode. Then I sprayed the bathroom so it didn't smell. There could be no signs left that anything had ever happened. Mama couldn't find out. I changed out of my clothes, hid them in the back of my closet, and put fresh clothes on. I closed the door, climbed into the bed, and cried myself to sleep.

I didn't wake up until Mama opened the door of my room and said, "Molly, why did you lock the back door? I couldn't get in, and why are you in the bed? It's just 3:30 in the afternoon." She didn't ask me if anything was wrong. What she did say was, "Paul and Tommy don't have keys to the house. You need to leave the door unlocked so they can get in."

"I'm sorry, Mama," I said. "I won't lock it anymore."

She closed the door and walked away. I halfway hoped that she would notice something, that she'd be curious enough to ask me if something was wrong, but she didn't. She was too tired from working all day.

Every Tuesday and Thursday, I started watching for Mr. Thompson's truck around 9:00 AM. I started watching for him early, although I knew he wouldn't be there until around 10:00 or 10:30. I was afraid he would come early and catch me off guard again, so I started watching for him an hour early. My daily routine stayed the same. When I saw his truck turn the corner heading toward my house, I ran to my room, locked the door, and slid under my bed. Always, I drew my legs to my chest and sucked my thumb. I whispered to myself over and over again,

"If I'm as quiet as a mouse, he won't know I'm here." But he knew I was there. He always came to my bedroom door and knocked. He would say, "Dolly, I know you're in there. I didn't mean to scare you, honey. Come on out and we'll talk the same way we used to. Come on out, Dolly, please. You didn't tell your Mama what happened, did you? You can't tell anyone what happened, Dolly. I don't want to hurt you. Everything will be fine. I promise."

For some reason, I knew that as long I was in my room, under my bed, he wasn't going to break the door down. He hadn't done it the first time and he wouldn't ever do it. He was more scared than I was that someone would find out.

Over the years, thinking back about Uncle Tea and Mr. Thompson and knowing what I know about other children who have been raped, it's easy to see that pedophiles pick you out and then work hard to gain your trust. I was a child who felt unloved, and I think both of them saw that, and so I was an easy target.

I remember an incident that happened one night not long after Mr. Thompson attacked me. I had fallen asleep on the floor in front of the TV, but I could hear my brothers laughing and I could sense that Daddy was annoyed. I could hear him saying, "Betty, get her up and take her to bed."

Mama was shaking me, trying to wake me up. "Molly, stop crying," she was saying. "You're okay. You're just having a nightmare." I was crawling around on the floor and crying, "He cut my thumb off, Mama. I can't find it."

Finally, when she was able to wake me, I put my arms around her neck and told her, "Mama, he cut my thumb off." Daddy, Paul, and Tommy laughed even harder. Not one of them, not even Mama, ever asked, "Who cut your thumb off?" Mama helped me to bed, and I remember lying there under the covers shivering and crying. I was scared to fall asleep.

When school started, the only time I was home was if I was sick, and I was sick a lot that year after it happened. I was extremely nervous, I had a hard time concentrating, and my grades went down. In school, I stayed to myself. I didn't try to make friends. My head was so crowded with the thoughts of guilt and shame, and I couldn't see my life ever being any better. I just wanted to disappear.

After Dr. J. read my journals, he told me that he was surprised I hadn't committed suicide when I was a young girl. Suicide never entered my mind, but running away from home did, and if I had had somewhere to run to and someone I could trust, I would have. But there was no one. I do believe, however, that I had a nervous breakdown that year after Mr. Thompson's attack. So much had happened and it was getting harder and harder for me to hide it. I started isolating myself from my family. I stayed in my bedroom with the door shut unless it was time to eat, and then I sat at the table with my head bowed and moved my food around the plate to make it appear that I was eating. I lost so much weight that Tommy started calling me "bone belly." Mama fussed at me for not eating, and Daddy fussed at me to eat so Mama would hush. At times, tears would roll down my cheeks and Mama would accuse Daddy of making me nervous, and so, as hard as I tried to keep from being the cause of their arguments, I was. When they were screaming at each other, I would sit in the bottom of my closet with the door shut trying not to hear them. Even that did no good.

Daddy and Mama got divorced again in August of 1963. They had been remarried for just two years when finally the fussing and the fighting and the screaming got to be too much. It consumed our lives. I wasn't sorry they were divorcing. I wasn't sorry that Daddy was leaving. I wasn't even sorry that we were having to move back to the Cracker Jack box. What I was sorry about was that they blamed the divorce on me. To quote the divorce complaint, "Complainant (Mama) avers that the defendant (Daddy) has cursed and abused the youngest child, Molly, on numerous occasions, and as a result she is in an extremely nervous condition and under a doctor's care and will soon be entered in St. Thomas Hospital as a result of his misconduct and treatment toward her." Of course, she stated that there were also other reasons for the divorce, but I was the main reason. I guess they had to blame it on somebody.

All I knew was that I would be free of Mr. Thompson. Nothing else mattered. We would be moving across town and I would never have to see him again. He wouldn't know where we went and I wouldn't have to be scared anymore. I was wrong.

Mr. Thompson followed us and delivered our milk wherever we lived. Mama never could get settled anywhere. In fact, between when we moved away from the farm when I was eight years old and I turned sixteen years old, we moved ten more times. Mama would rent out the Cracker Jack box to other people and we would rent other houses in town. We never settled down in one house for very long until we moved again. Nowhere was home.

Wherever we moved, Mr. Thompson made sure he found us and delivered our milk, and I always wondered why. Surely after a while, he had to know that I wasn't going to tell anyone what he did to me. I guess he felt like he needed to constantly remind me that he knew where I was and would always be watching me. The thing was that I didn't want anybody to know any more than he did. He just didn't know that.

After that day of the attack, I never laid eyes on Mr. Thompson again. I was always in my room with the door locked and hiding under my bed when he came into the house. He never failed to call out for me, and if no one was home, he continued to walk through whatever house we lived in looking for me. I felt like a prisoner in my own home, and I guess that was his plan. He was going to make sure that I never told on him.

I've talked a lot about being in fear for the four years Mr. Thompson stalked me, but fear can't even begin to describe what I felt. The worst kind of terror consumed me every day. I was hunted just like an animal, knowing that any minute my life could be over. I knew that if he ever was able to catch me, he wouldn't just rape me again; the next time he would kill me.

MR. CRAFT

When I was twelve years old, after Mr. Thompson's rape and while Daddy still lived with us, I started babysitting to earn spending money. Most of the girls my age were doing this. The going rate was $.50 an hour, and for the two to three hours I was there, I made $2.00 to $3.00. It doesn't seem like much money now, but it was a lot for a young girl to have in her pocket back then.

The first family who called me to babysit was the Burtons. They were a young couple who had a small baby girl, just three months old. It's the first time I had been around a small baby, and although I was excited to get the job, I agreed to do it only on the condition that Mama went with me. I felt unsure about keeping such a small baby and was afraid that somehow she might get hurt. Every week, before the weekend ever arrived, I started hoping they would call me. Not only did I look forward to being with the baby and earning money, but it was a nice break from Mama and Daddy's fighting.

After I had been babysitting with the Burtons for a while, I was called by another family, the Crafts. They were also a young couple, in their late twenties or early thirties, and had two small children, a girl five years old and a two-year-old boy. Mrs. Craft was beautiful. She was tall and had blonde hair and blue eyes, and I'd never seen a woman dress so prettily. Mr. Craft was tall, handsome, and built like an athlete. They made a beautiful couple. When this job came up, I didn't ask Mama to go with me. I wanted to do it all on my own without her help, and so I always went alone. Once I started babysitting for them, they called me almost every weekend.

I had been sitting for them on a regular basis for about a month or so when Mrs. Craft called me one Saturday night to babysit. They were going to a party and said they would be home pretty late, and that was okay with me. The later they stayed out, the more money I made.

It was well after midnight when they arrived home. When they came in, I could tell something was wrong with them. Although I had never been around anyone who drank liquor, I knew they had been drinking because of the way they talked and moved. Each time I babysat for the Crafts, Mrs. Craft had always picked me up and driven me back home, but that night Mr. Craft insisted that he'd drive me home. It had been snowing all day and the roads were iced over. As soon as he volunteered to do it, I was consumed with fear. He had never given me any reason to be afraid of him, but then I had never had to be alone with him either.

As we walked out of the house and to the car, Mr. Craft took hold of my arm to help me to the car, and just the touch of his hand on me sent my whole body into a panic mode. Instantly I jerked away from him. It surprised him, but he didn't say anything. He opened the car door for me, and as I slid in and he shut the door behind me, my instinct told me that I was in trouble and needed to run, but instead I froze up and sat there scared to death to move. The air in the car was filled with the stench of liquor and was even worse when he turned his head to talk to me.

On the drive home, Mr. Craft made small talk about the children, asking me if they had behaved well, and with each question he asked, I answered strictly "yes" or "no," trying to avoid friendly conversation with him. He had always been nice to me, and even though I felt a little silly being so scared, my past experience in trusting men had warned me to be on guard. The Crafts lived in a neighborhood behind me, just one street over, but because of the snow, the drive home seemed to last forever.

As soon as we turned down my street and before Mr. Craft ever pulled into my driveway, I took hold of the door handle, prepared to jump out as soon as he stopped the car. My intuition had been right. As soon as he stopped the car I tried to step out, but I was held back. Mr. Craft had his arm around my shoulder, pulling me toward him. My heart started pounding so hard that I couldn't breathe, and I froze. He started out by asking me how old I was, and then he started stroking the back of my hair, telling me how beautiful it was. I didn't know what I was going to do. I tried to pull away from him without looking at him, but he just held me that much tighter.

Finally I looked into his eyes for only an instant before I pushed him away and screamed, "Leave me alone!" I flung the door open, stepped out of the car, and ran as fast as I could through the snow toward the back door of my house, not knowing if he was coming after me or not. As I rounded the corner, I heard him shout at me, and for an instant, I glanced back at him. He was standing just outside his car door.

"Molly, you forgot your money," he shouted, waving it at me. "Come back."

I never slowed down, not until I was safe inside my house with the door locked behind me. I listened and I watched, and finally I saw the headlights of his car backing away from my house. Then I slid down on my hands and knees to the floor and cried. As I always did, I went over and over in my mind what I had done to cause his attack. I had not been nice to Mr. Craft. I had never talked to him except to answer a question. I gave him no reason to hurt me. But I knew that somehow I had done something to cause it.

There was not a sound in the house. Although they had left a light on for me, no one had even stayed up to make sure I got home safe. I was just twelve years old. Why didn't anyone worry about me?

I barely slept that night, slipping off into a nap only to be awakened by the racing of my heart and the racing thoughts going through my mind. The next morning when Mama came into my room, I was already awake but acted like I had been in a deep sleep all night. I couldn't let her see what a nervous state I was in. She told me that Mrs. Craft had just come to the house and dropped my money off. She laid $5.00 on my bedside table. Although it was double what I should have been paid, I didn't want the money.

"You must have been pretty tired last night when you got home," Mama said. "You didn't even give Mr. Craft time to pay you."

I looked at the money but didn't answer her. She didn't ask me anything about the night before, and although I halfway hoped she would, I knew I wouldn't have told her what happened anyway. I lay in the bed for a long while going over and over what happened and knew there was only one thing to do.

Finally I got up, took the scissors from Mama's sewing basket, and locked myself in the bathroom. I cut one long strand of my hair on the side of my head and watched as it fell to the floor. My hair was like silk, long, black, and shiny, and hung down to the center of my back. It was the one thing, the only thing, anyone ever complimented me about. Mama had always told me that I looked like Elizabeth Taylor when she starred in *Black Beauty*. But I wasn't stupid. I knew if I resembled Elizabeth Taylor at all, it was only because of my hair.

I stood in front of the mirror and looked at myself. I was going to make a horrible mess, and Mama was going to be so mad at me. I didn't want to upset her. She had enough going on without that, so I took the scissors to her and showed her what I had done.

Immediately she yelled, "What did you do?"

I told her simply, "My hair's too long. I want you to cut it."

For the first time in my life, I didn't care what Mama thought. I had come to realize that the only person who was going to protect me was me, and I had to do whatever it took to do that. Getting rid of my hair was just the start.

I thought Mama was going to cry. She just couldn't believe what I had done. She didn't ask me if anything was wrong, but she had no reason to. I had gotten really good at hiding my feelings and the fear I was feeling inside. If she wondered at all if there was something serious going on with me, she didn't ask. It was almost like Mama walked around in a daze in her own little world. Like me, it seemed that she went through the regular, daily routines of life, just hoping she'd get through the day without something bad happening. The only thing that seemed to shake her was when Daddy came through the door. Then the fighting started. Sometimes it seemed to me that Mama and Daddy enjoyed fighting with each other. They gave no thought to what it was doing to me or to my brothers.

At first Mama adamantly refused to cut my hair, but then she realized that she had no choice. She had to straighten out the mess I had made.

When she was finished, Tommy made fun of me while Paul looked at me in disbelief. Daddy said nothing. Mama had tried her best to cut my hair in some sort of style, but it was hopeless. When she had done all she could do, I finally looked in the mirror. I wanted to cry, but I didn't dare. I couldn't believe what I had done to myself, but it was okay, because now they would leave me alone. There was nothing about me that was pretty anymore.

Mrs. Craft called me to babysit several times after that night, but I always gave her an excuse. I never babysat for them again. I refused to babysit for the Burtons too. It was the last time I took any babysitting job. Making the money not only gave me plenty of money to spend, but it gave me a sense of pride and maturity; and more than anything else, I finally felt like I had control over some part of my life. But it wasn't worth it. There was already too much in my life haunting me. I couldn't take anymore, not for a few dollars.

To this day, I still can't imagine why Mr. Craft came on to me, except that he'd been drinking; but that was no excuse. Both Mr. Thompson and Mr. Craft were nice men with nice families. They had to know that I might tell on them and that if I did, they risked losing everything. Even I knew that.

I never saw Mr. Craft again after that night, and many years later, after I had gotten married, I heard that he died. He was still a young man, maybe in his forties. He was playing golf at the local country club and dropped dead from a massive heart attack. I felt sad for him and for his family. As with most of the people in my life who had hurt me, I wished Mr. Craft would die. I actually prayed for it, and it was wrong. He had scared me, but he had not hurt me, not like the others. To wish death on him, on anyone, was wrong.

MY GREATEST FEAR

When Mama and Daddy divorced in 1963, Mama had it written in the divorce complaint that "defendant (Daddy) has cursed and abused the youngest child, Molly, on numerous occasions, and as a result she is in an extremely nervous condition and under a doctor's care and will soon be entered in St. Thomas Hospital as a result of his misconduct and treatment toward her."

I didn't find the decree until after Mama died and I had to go through her things. I was pretty shocked that she actually blamed me for the divorce. I don't remember Daddy cursing me or abusing me, although I do remember him fussing at me at the dinner table when Mama insisted that I clean my plate and I couldn't. I also remember his angry explosions when Mama would tell him how nervous the fighting was making me, but mostly the explosions were directed at Mama when they were fighting over the farm and over money and over anything else they could think of that only involved their problems, not mine. The fighting never seemed to bother my brothers. If it did, they didn't let it show. I do remember Paul defending Mama when Daddy would act like he was going to hit her. I don't remember Daddy ever hitting Mama, although he did push her around quite a bit during their arguments. I was always so scared that he would hurt her that, a lot of times, I stood by and waited, prepared to help her if he did.

Mama had no idea why I was so nervous. She didn't know about

Uncle Tea or Mr. Thompson or Mr. Craft. She had never realized what Kathy's death had done to me, either. She, and everyone else around me, was so oblivious to what was happening to me.

The first real signs of my condition started showing up when I started my period at twelve years old. The bleeding started and wouldn't stop. After ten days of heavy bleeding, Mama took me to the doctor, whom I will refer to as Dr. B. He decided to put me in St. Thomas Hospital for testing. Both he and Mama thought it was because of my nerves. Mama told him about Daddy and his explosions and was sure he was the reason for my condition. When we came home from the doctor that day Mama told Daddy that he had to move out.

They might have blamed it on me, but in my heart, I knew that the separation wasn't because of me. I figured that Daddy would only be out of the house for a short period of time, just long enough for the bleeding to stop and for me to get well. All it did was give Daddy reason to hate me more. I could see it in his eyes.

I went into the hospital immediately after Daddy moved out. The doctor did all kind of tests on me but never told me his findings. Still I continued to bleed, and finally they started giving me pints of blood. I lost a lot of weight and became really weak from not eating. Although she never said it, I knew Mama was scared I was going to die. I probably would have been better off if Mama hadn't stayed at the hospital with me because all she did was cry and pray and so I knew my condition was bad.

One day, several days after I had arrived there and after all the tests were done, the doctor sent the nurse in for Mama and they left the room. About an hour later, the doctor, Mama, and a man I had never seen came back into the room. They were standing on either side of Mama, holding her up under the arms, helping her to walk. Mama had been crying and her face was swollen. Neither of them spoke a word, but I could see the dread in their eyes and I knew they were fixing to tell me I was going to die.

A sudden rush of relief came over me. It's hard to explain, but I did feel relieved. My life would be over. I wouldn't have to live in constant fear anymore. No one would ever be able to hurt me again, and finally I could be at peace.

Mama stood at the foot of the bed holding on to keep from falling while both the doctor and the man I didn't know stood on each side of my bed. I wasn't at all afraid. I knew that I could take whatever was coming, but I wasn't prepared for what Dr. B. did say.

In a calm voice, he said, "You're hurt up inside, Molly. Someone's hurt you pretty bad. You need to tell me who." My greatest fear had finally happened.

I drew my breath in, my heart started pounding, and I looked at him in shock and disbelief. He had examined me up inside, and the day he did I was horrified. He had explained what he was going to do before he did it, and although it was uncomfortable, he didn't hurt me. Just the same, I cried all the way through it. Just knowing that a man was going to be down there touching me was almost more than I could bear. Mama had talked to me about my period and told me what to expect when I started bleeding, but the birds and the bees, womanhood, and anything relating to it had never been discussed. While Dr. B. was examining me, all I could think about was Uncle Tea and his long, nasty fingernails. It had felt like he was cutting gashes up inside me with a knife, and I remembered the terrible pain and the bleeding. But there was no way Dr. B. could know what he did. How could he possibly know?

When I looked away from Dr. B. and didn't answer him, again he asked me who it was that hurt me. Still I didn't say a word. He introduced the man standing on the other side of my bed as someone who was there to help me.

"Whoever it is that hurt you, Molly," he said, "might hurt another little girl too. Do you want that to happen?"

His remark made me so angry, and I wanted to say to him, "Why would I ever want that to happen?" I already knew that it was possible, but what was I supposed to do? I wanted my family to love me. If they found out, they wouldn't.

So I told the man innocently and to the point, "No one has hurt me."

He continued to talk to me about men, about sex, and about what they do to little girls to hurt them. He told me that whoever hurt me was an evil man and that unless he was stopped, he would hurt other children. I listened to him intently as he explained rape, and for the first time I understood what had been done to me and why. He went on to tell me that what happened was not my fault, and although I wanted so bad to believe him, I couldn't. At the same time, I knew the fault was not only mine but it was Mama's and it was Mammie's too. They were the ones who trusted Uncle Tea to take care of me.

When the man was finished with what he had to say, I looked at Mama. She was still standing at the end of my bed holding on as tightly as she could. She looked at the wall above my head and tears were streaming down her cheeks. She wouldn't look at me. I was sure it was because she was ashamed of me. As bad as I wanted to cry, I held it back. If I cried, I would give myself away for sure. Both Dr. B. and the man continued to talk to me, trying to convince me to tell, but it was hopeless. I wasn't going to tell them. I would never tell anyone.

Finally Dr. B. looked at Mama and said, "She's not going to tell us who did it, Mrs. Williams."

Then he looked at me again and said, "Molly, I'm going to try and fix you, but you may never be able to have children."

"It's okay," I told him. "I don't want any children."

That's when Mama couldn't hold it anymore. She started sobbing, and when I looked at her, she looked at me and just as quickly looked away. There was so much sorrow in her eyes. I had never wanted to hurt Mama. I had done everything I knew to do to keep her from finding out, but she knew what the doctor told her was the truth.

I was okay with the fact that I would never have children. I wouldn't ever want anyone to hurt my child, not like I was hurt, and I knew that no matter how hard I tried to protect her, eventually someone would hurt her or she would die, like Kathy did. Getting married and having children was something I never planned to do. I couldn't wait to grow up and escape the life I was living.

Finally Mama and the two men left my room. An hour later, Mama came back. She was pushing a wheelchair. Although her face was still swollen, she had stopped crying. Instead she had a fake smile plastered on her face.

"Come on, Molly," she said in a happy voice. "Let's go get ice cream."

She rolled me down to the cafeteria and we sat quietly and ate our ice cream. Mama never mentioned what was said. She asked me no questions and made no attempt to try to get me to confess. I bled for fifty straight days and stayed in the hospital for weeks until Dr. B. felt like I was strong enough to go home. I continued to bleed even after I was released from the hospital. Paul carried me from the bed to the couch and from the couch to the bathroom. I wasn't allowed to stand up or walk, even if I wanted to.

When the bleeding stopped and I got my strength back, we moved back to our little house across town, the Cracker Jack box. Daddy had moved back to the farm before I went into the hospital. If Mama told him I was there, he never came to see me and he never called me to see how I was feeling, but it was probably just as well. My nerves calmed down after he left. The constant screaming and the fighting were over, and I hoped to be rid of Mr. Thompson too, once we moved. Everything had happened for the best. It was just too good to be true.

Mama never mentioned to me again what the doctor told her. If she told Daddy or anyone what they suspected, nothing was ever said. I have to think that it was too much for her to comprehend. She had lost Kathy to cancer, and the thought of losing me too was more than she could bear. And just maybe she didn't want to know who did it. After all, the only men she knew of who were ever around me were Daddy and my brothers. What if it was one of them? What would she do? She must have thought it was better if she didn't know. That's what I tell myself anyway. I'm sure she never gave a thought to Uncle Tea or Mr. Thompson.

I never knew who the man was who came into my room that day with Dr. B. He wasn't a policeman because he was dressed in plain clothes. He could have been a social worker, but he wasn't introduced as such. He was just a man who, supposedly, was there to help me. Whoever he was, he never came to see me again. I had been raped. They knew that, but they didn't pursue it, and to this day I wonder why. Maybe it was at Mama's insistence. Maybe they thought my condition was too fragile and it was better to let it alone. Maybe they were convinced that I'd never tell no matter how much they begged. Whatever the reason, no further questions were ever asked, not by Mama, not by anyone.

The day of my wedding, when I was twenty-one, Mama was helping me with my wedding dress when she abruptly said, "Bobby's gonna know that someone else has touched you. Tell him the doctor did it when he examined you. That's all you have to say."

And there it was, short and to the point.

I never answered her and it was never mentioned again.

VALERIE

You would think that by the time I turned fourteen years old and had had so much happen to me I'd have been prepared to face anything else that came along, but that wasn't the case. Never would I have been prepared to face what happened to Valerie.

I had been a student at St. John's for several years before Valerie started coming to school there. She was a year younger than me, but because there were three grades in one classroom, she and I were in the same room and under the same teacher. I remember the very first time I saw her. It was obvious that she had never gone to a Catholic school. It was the first day of school and any child who had ever gone there knew that once you walked through those thick double doors into the school, there was to be no talking, no running, and no laughter. There was to be no sign of self-expression. We were there strictly to learn and to obey.

Most of the children were already seated when Valerie came bouncing into the room, her eyes wide with excitement. Everyone stared at her in amazement. Who was this girl who dared to be happy? She definitely wasn't one of us. The rest of us were like tiny soldiers marching in place, speaking only when spoken to. We watched her as she raced around the room, up one row and down the other, trying to decide what desk she wanted. She got away with it only because the nun had not come into the room, and as I watched her, I wondered just how long it would take the nuns to break her. I had been easy for them. My spirit had been broken years before I got there.

Valerie was cute but not what you would call pretty. She was short and stocky and muscular for a girl. She was the first tomboy I had ever known. Unlike the others girls in class, she had a waistline, hips, and breasts and was built more like a woman than a young girl eleven or twelve years old. She had long, shiny auburn hair that flowed down the middle of her back but that she usually wore up in a ponytail. When she smiled, it was noticeable that one of her two front teeth was badly chipped. The one thing that stands out in my mind about Valerie was how happy she was. Like my brother Tommy, she was a teaser, the girl who always had something funny to say to make everyone laugh, the girl everyone wanted to be friends with. I don't remember ever seeing her down, even when the nuns disciplined her with words or with the ruler across her knuckles. She just laughed about it, and because of her easy-going temperament, it wasn't long before we knew that the nuns favored her over the rest of us. They gave up very quickly on trying to tame her.

Valerie was the third child in a family of five children. She had two older sisters, a younger brother, and a younger sister, and like my family, they didn't seem to be very well off. Up until Valerie started to attend school at St. John's, I felt like I was the only girl in school who was poor, who didn't have nice clothes. Valerie seemed to be the only girl, other than me, who wore hand-me-down clothes, and by the time her clothes were handed down to her from her two older sisters, they were pretty worn. Everything I wore was also second-hand, either from a thrift store or from a cousin who was six years older than me. Never did I wear anything in style. I was so envious of the other girls and at the same time embarrassed and humiliated, but nothing embarrassed Valerie.

I remember one dress in particular that she wore more than most. It was beige with tiny pink flowers. It had a small round collar and short puffy sleeves and the hemline extended right below her knees. I can still see her bouncing around school in that dress. Never before then or since have I had a friend who was so completely happy and content with who she was.

Because she was a good athlete, she was the only girl ever asked by the boys to play baseball at play period, and she could hit, run, and catch better than any boy in the school. Although she put them all to shame, each team still fought over who would get Valerie.

After the eighth grade, I graduated from St. John's and moved on to the local public high school. Valerie would have been in the eighth grade, but she left St. John's that same year and went to the public junior high school so she could play basketball and became a star on the team very quickly. I wasn't surprised. The only time I saw her after that year was after church on Sunday, and from time to time we talked on the telephone. We had spent several years together at St. John's, and as with most of the students who went there, we had bonded over the years and made friendships that would last a lifetime.

The fall had come and gone that year and winter had set in. Thanksgiving, Christmas, and New Year's had passed. It was the year 1966. I had turned fifteen on January 28. Valerie was to turn fourteen in February. It had been snowing for weeks, and school had been closed because the roads were so treacherous. The snow stood several feet deep and icicles hung from the tree limbs, making it the winter wonderland that was always described in Christmas songs.

Valerie had started babysitting on the weekends to earn spending money. She had been babysitting for some time for the Colliers, a prominent young couple in town. One night, the Colliers were invited to a party in town and Valerie was called to sit with their two small children. I'm sure that Valerie had gone through the same routine all of us went through when we babysat. She probably played games, ate snacks, and read to the children before finally putting them to bed. Who knows what time she drifted off to sleep in front of the television set?

Mr. Collier, who was twenty-seven years old, had been talking with a group of men at the party when he left them, found his wife, and gave her the excuse that he felt ill and was going home. This is the story he told the police that night. A simple story but so horrifying.

It was between 9:00 and 10:00 PM when he left the party. When he arrived home, he found Valerie's naked body lying on the floor in the living room, and there was a man standing over her with a gun. Mr. Collier described him as being a white man of normal build and well dressed. He said the man ordered him to pick Valerie up and carry her to his car. He was then ordered to drive across town to the rear of the local bowling alley where a late-model white car was parked. He told Mr. Collier to transfer Valerie's body to that car, and once he had, the man drove away with Valerie. He said the man drove off in the direction of the Cumberland Bridge, which is approximately four miles out of town. Mr. Collier said that he immediately returned home but told police that he did not call them right away because he was too scared. Sometime between 12:30 and 12:45 AM, his wife returned home from the party and the police were notified.

Mr. Collier told the police about the man he found with Valerie and what he had been made to do. Upon examination, the police found that Mr. Collier's clothes were soaked with blood. The rear seat of his car was also covered with blood. Upon further examination, they found blood on Mr. Collier's underwear.

The search for Valerie started immediately. They started the search at the bowling alley where he had last seen the man and Valerie and proceeded all the way out to the Cumberland Bridge. Without any luck, the officer's decided to walk across the bridge. When nothing was found on the front side of the bridge, they continued to walk across the bridge to see if any clues could be found. As they reached the far side, they found a pair of girls' panties caught on the bridge railing, a blood-soaked scarf, and a button lying on the road. When these pieces of clothing were shown to Valerie's mother, she identified them as belonging to Valerie.

It had been approximately four hours after Valerie's murder when the police had been called. Civil defense workers were called out long before daylight to begin dragging the river for her body. Although they were hampered by the ice and severe cold, they dragged the river all day and into the next evening until finally Valerie's body was pulled from the river. Mr. Collier was charged with Valerie's rape and murder.

At his arraignment, he pled not guilty. At his trial, however, he admitted that he was the one who killed Valerie. He said that upon arriving at his home that night, he found Valerie asleep in a chair in front of the TV set. He then went to his children's bedrooms, checked on them to make sure they were asleep, and then closed their bedroom doors. He went to the chair where Valerie was sleeping and shot her in the head with his gun. He then pulled her body to the floor, stripped her of her clothes, and raped her. Afterward, he rolled her body up into the rug she was lying on and carried her to his car where he placed her in the back seat. He then drove to the Cumberland Bridge and threw her body into the river. When the autopsy was performed on Valerie's body, it was determined that she was still alive when she was thrown into those frozen, icy waters. Her lungs were full of water.

The morning after Valerie was murdered, Mama woke me up as soon as she saw the news on TV. I sat and listened as the broadcaster related the story of her murder. A picture of Valerie came up on the screen. There she was with that huge smile on her face, the broken tooth visible. The bridge was shown and also the boats below with men dragging the river for her body. Mr. Collier was shown being carried into the local jail.

I sat on the floor in front of the TV and watched in disbelief. How could he have hurt Valerie? It was hard to zero in on everything the broadcaster was saying because my mind was filled with so many thoughts. So many questions started running through my mind as I watched the story unfold. Was she awake when he shot her? Had she felt the bullet blasting away at her brain? Did she know she was being raped? Was she conscious enough to be terrified? When she hit those frozen waters, did she know she was drowning? I wanted so much to talk to Mama about what had happened to Valerie, but when the newscaster stated that Valerie was raped, I knew that I couldn't. What if I gave myself away? It would be so easy. I didn't dare let Mama see the tears that rolled down my cheeks or the horror in my face. I got up and went to my bedroom, shutting the door behind me. There I covered my face with a pillow to muffle the sounds of screaming.

I didn't know the Colliers except that Valerie babysat for them. They lived just off the main street in town in an older neighborhood. Their house was a huge, red-brick, two-story home that had been built in the late 1800s. The house has been boarded up for years and has looked as though it's about ready to fall down, but just recently, driving past it, I noticed that someone was fixing it up. The boards over the windows were taken down and it has been freshly painted. The yard has been mowed and fresh landscaping has been set in. It's hard to believe that anyone would want to live in that house knowing that a young girl had been raped and murdered there, so I have to believe that the people who live there don't know it. I had hoped for years that the house would burn down as I'm sure most people in town had, but it still stands forty years later, and now it's been brought back to life.

Up until the time when Valerie was murdered, I had never known of another child being raped. I had never heard anyone talk about it nor had I seen anything on television or the news about it. I figured I was probably the only girl it had been done to and it had happened to me because I had been naive and trusting. That morning, as I listened to the news, I knew why it happened to Valerie. She had been nice to Mr. Collier, and that's all it took.

I'm sure Mr. Collier killed Valerie so she wouldn't tell on him. At that moment, I realized how lucky I was to be alive, but I also realized that both Uncle Tea and Mr. Thompson were still out there and lived no more than a thirty-minute drive from me. They would be watching the news too and would see what Mr. Collier had done to keep Valerie quiet. I became frantic at the thought that either one, or both of them, might come after me. I could still tell on them, and they knew it. Although I was filled with so much sadness for Valerie, fear for my own safety consumed me. It had been six years since I had seen Uncle Tea. I wasn't as afraid of him as I was Mr. Thompson. He hadn't threatened to hurt me.

It was freezing outside and the snow was coming down hard, but I had to get out of the house. I had to clear my thoughts and think of what I should do to save myself. I started walking in circles round and round and round the backyard, and I talked to God. If he was listening, as mama always said he always was, then surely he would hear me, so once again I begged him to help me. I begged him to tell me what to do. I had no one else.

I knew I needed to talk to Mama, but once again it ran through my mind what Uncle Tea had said to me: "If they find out you were nasty, they won't love you anymore." I still believed it to be true. As I paced the backyard that morning and thought about the three men, I felt responsible for what happened to Valerie. I should have warned her. I should have told her about Uncle Tea and Mr. Thompson and I should have told her about Mr. Craft too. If I had, she might still be alive. I could have warned her, warned all of my friends, about men. I could have begged them not to babysit, but if I did, what questions would they ask me? Would I be able to answer their questions without giving myself away? It just never entered my mind that anyone would hurt them. They weren't like me. They weren't shy and withdrawn, and they had people who cared about them, people who were concerned about their safety.

I had been having bad nightmares for years, but after Valerie's death, they worsened. Every night in my sleep, I would see her down in the water, naked, panic in her eyes, her mouth open, screaming and begging me to help her. But I couldn't help her. I was in those frozen waters too, begging her to help me.

It had been a couple of days after Valerie's death and it was time to go to the funeral home. Mama told me to me to get ready, but I told her, "I'm not going."

She came back at me with, "Of course you're going." It wasn't up for discussion.

"I don't want to go, Mama. Please don't make me," I begged, but there was to be no arguing. Things had to be Mama's way or no way.

"You have to pay your respects," she said.

"Valerie was my friend, Mama," I said. "I don't want to see her." I choked back the tears as best I could. Kathy had been the only person I had ever known to die, and I could still see her lying in that coffin. The thought of seeing Valerie like that made me feel like my head was going to explode.

"You're going," she said. "Get ready." And that was that. She wasn't going to change her mind. I wanted so much to scream at her, but I never had. Screaming at her would be a mortal sin. God would never forgive me. I gave in and got dressed.

When we arrived at the funeral home, the crowds had already gathered. People were lined up from the back of the building all the way around to the front, waiting to get inside. I couldn't understand why anyone would want to see Valerie in that shape. It felt disrespectful to me. Seeing Kathy lying in her casket had never left me, and it's not the way I wanted to remember Valerie. Why would they?

We waited in line for what seemed to be an hour outside in the freezing cold. Everybody in the line was talking, each of them giving their version of how Valerie was murdered. I just wanted them to shut up. Did any of them know what she had gone through? Did they even have a clue?

Slowly but surely, the line became shorter and shorter until we were finally inside the front door. Just in the next room, I could see Valerie's parents, her sisters, and her brother sitting just on the other side of the casket. People were moving slowly past them, shaking their hands. I started feeling the sensation of ants running through my body, and I remembered what Daddy had told me when we stood over Kathy's casket: "Don't touch her. She's asleep. She's well now." He had lied to me. She wasn't well. She was dead and she was never coming back. This time, I knew going into that room that Valerie was dead and she wasn't coming back. I made my mind up that I wouldn't look at her. I would keep my eyes closed.

The closer I got to the casket, the more nervous I got. I started sweating, even though it was so cold in the room, and everything around me started going in circles. All I could see were spots in front of me, and I felt like if I didn't sit down, I would fall down. I grabbed hold of Mama's dress when she turned to me and said, "All you have to do is tell her mother that you're sorry."

When the casket was in clear view, I kept my eyes to the ground and held onto Mama that much tighter. She might have made me come to the funeral, but the one thing she couldn't do was make me look at Valerie, and I was determined not to.

When Mama finally stood in front of the coffin, she turned to me and said, "Molly, it's okay. Just remember that Valerie's not in any pain. She's in heaven now."

I held onto Mama's dress and pressed my body up against her. I tried not to look at Valerie, but then Mama pulled away from me. She left me standing there alone, in front of the casket, and I was frozen. I couldn't move. I glanced inside the coffin. There was a woman lying in the casket, but it wasn't Valerie. It was someone I didn't know. We were in the wrong room. We had to be. I looked at Valerie's mother and back at the woman lying in the casket. I looked the woman over from her face down to her hands, and then I recognized it. It was her dress; the pink, flowered dress. The dress I had seen Valerie wear so many times. I looked from the dress back to the face, but it wasn't Valerie lying there. There had to be a mistake. It just couldn't be Valerie. I was looking at an older woman with short, chopped-off hair all curled up and teased, the way Mama wore hers. The woman had makeup on and lipstick. Valerie's hair was long and shiny, and Valerie would never have worn makeup or lipstick. But that was her dress, so it had to be Valerie I was looking at. The young, vibrant girl so full of life that I knew was gone. She had been replaced with someone I didn't recognize.

Valerie's body was so swollen from being down in the river so long. I stood there and stared at her, unable to move or speak, and Then I saw it—the huge hole in her temple where he had shot her. They had tried to cover it up, but it was too large and too deep to conceal with makeup. Look what he had done to her. I couldn't believe it.

As I stared at Valerie, everyone and every sound in the room seemed to fade away. Valerie and I were all alone in the room, and I started talking to her. I told her how sorry I was that I didn't warn her. I tried to explain my reasons for not telling her. I couldn't give myself away. Suddenly I felt Mama shaking me and telling me to stop. "Everyone's looking," she said.

I looked from Valerie to her mother, from Valerie to her sisters, and back at Valerie, and then the room started spinning and I felt Mama catch me as I started to fall. "I'm sorry," I was screaming. "I'm sorry, I'm sorry."

I looked at Mama and then looked around the room. Everyone had stopped talking. Everyone was looking at me. I looked at Valerie's mother once again, wiped my eyes, and as softly as I could, I told her, "I'm sorry." I turned and ran from the room, through the front door, and out of the building. I didn't look at anybody. I just ran.

When I finally found our car, I waited there for Mama, and when she approached me I started screaming at her, "Why did you make me come, Mama? I begged you not to make me come. Why did you make me come? That could be me lying in there, Mama. Don't you know that?"

"That's not you in there," she screamed back at me. "I would never let something like that happen to you." I looked at her in disbelief. She knew something had happened to me. Dr. B. told her that somebody had hurt me. That day in my hospital room, when I was twelve years old, Dr. B. had told her, right in front of me, that someone had hurt me pretty bad. She had left the room that day and never mentioned it again. It was as though it had never happened.

"Mama, look at me," I screamed at her. "That could be me lying in there, Mama. You know that."

At that very moment, I finally saw it in her face. She knew it was true. She just didn't want to admit that something like that could happen to one of her children. I halfway hoped that the wall that stood between us would come down and that she would say to me, "I know it could be you. Tell me who hurt you. Tell me now so I can help you."

But it just wasn't in her. Without saying another word, she looked away from me, opened the car door, and said, "Let's go home."

When we were both seated in the car, I turned to her and said very calmly, "You'll never make me do something I don't want to do again, Mama, never." She didn't look at me and didn't answer me.

Mama and I didn't talk on the way home, nor did we talk the rest of the night. The next few days came and went, and so did Valerie's funeral; going to it was never mentioned. That night was the first time I had ever screamed at my mother, the first time that I had ever stood my ground with her. I knew I had committed a sin according to the Catholic religion, but it had to be done. On Sunday I didn't confess my sin to the priest. I had already talked to God and told him I was sorry. I had to hope he understood. I had to hope he forgave me.

Things changed between me and Mama after that night. There was an unspoken understanding between us. I was allowed to have a say-so in decisions that involved me, and when I was adamant about not wanting to do certain things, she didn't make me.

People continued talking about Valerie's death for a long time, as long as it took for the trial to be over. Mr. Collier was sent to prison for life, but at least he was allowed to live. He had killed Valerie. There would be no more life for her, and for what, five minutes of sick pleasure!

In my whole life, I don't think I've ever quite known anyone else like Valerie. She was such a free spirit. There seemed to be nothing that could bring her down, and I think that's why I liked her so much. I just enjoyed being in her presence. I felt good about myself when I was. I would watch her and wish I were her, but I knew I never could be.

I have come to know things about myself. I always look on the negative side of life, never expecting anything good to happen to me, and when it does, I feel guilty and know I don't deserve it. I have always understood why men hurt me. I was shy and withdrawn and a perfect target, but I'll never in my lifetime understand why it happened to Valerie.

When I got my license, a year later after Valerie's death, one of the first places I drove to was her grave. I knelt down beside it and talked to her. I told her how sorry I was that I hadn't warned her. I could have warned her about men without telling her what happened to me. It would have been so simple. The guilt of that has stayed with me my whole life. I often wonder what she would be like today, if she would have children, if we would still be friends.

Every now and then I am forced to drive over the Cumberland Bridge, and miles before I ever reach it, Valerie always comes to mind. As I gaze into the waters below, I pray that she was not aware of what was happening to her that night. The medical examiner said she was alive when he threw her into that river, but I pray that she wasn't. I pray that she's at peace.

HE'S BACK

The fall I was supposed to start my freshmen year in high school, we moved to Hendersonville, a neighboring town. Tommy had been on the football team at Gallatin High School and was one of the star players. He had gotten caught drinking and was kicked off the team. When the coach in Hendersonville found out about it, he called Mama and offered Tommy a position on their team; for Tommy's sake, there was nothing else to be done but move. I cried and I begged, but there was no changing Mama's mind. I had graduated from St. John's and had made new friends over the summer, and for the first time in my life I was excited about starting school. None of that mattered. We had to do what was best for Tommy, and once again Mama thought the move would be good for us. In six short years, we had already moved eight times.

In less than a week, Mama found us another house and we packed up and moved. We moved into a rundown duplex directly across the street from the school, and for the first time in my life, I was actually embarrassed about where I lived. We had not even settled in before school started, and once again I had to start making new friends. That had always been hard for me because of my feelings of inferiority. I had never warmed up to people very easily. I was cautious about who I let into my life.

Almost immediately, Tommy became popular with everyone in the school. He was so cute and had so much personality, and I knew that the girls who tried to make friends with me only wanted to so they could get close to him. I resented everything about Tommy. He was everything I wanted to be but never could be.

After we had lived in the duplex for a few months, Mama decided she didn't like it. She found a house in a decent neighborhood, and once again we moved. Since the move from Gallatin, I had not seen Mr. Thompson. No matter where we moved, Mr. Thompson had always found us and had continued to stalk me. I was always in my room with the door locked and under my bed and he always had come to the door and tried to talk me out, warning me of what he would do if I told on him. My life was hell. I knew that eventually he would catch me off guard and he would kill me. He had too much to lose if I told on him.

After the move to Hendersonville and after seven months had passed, I finally started feeling relieved. He wasn't going to find us, not this time. I would see Thompson's Milk Company trucks in town from time to time, and I was always watchful, trying to see if he was driving one of them, but he never was. I assumed that Hendersonville wasn't his delivery area and I was free of him. Still I never let go of the fact that he was still out there somewhere and that no matter what I had to be on guard. I stayed in constant fear that someday he'd find me.

One night that summer, we were sitting in the kitchen eating supper when there was a knock at the back door. When Mama opened it, there he stood. It was Mr. Thompson. I couldn't believe it. He had found me. My heart started pounding and my throat tightened up and I looked down at my plate of food, scared to death to look at him. I had not seen his face since that first day he molested me. I had always been hidden.

"Well, I've finally found you," he told Mama. "You left without saying goodbye." He looked at my brothers and said, "Hey, boys."

"And there's Dolly," he said. "Still as pretty as ever."

I never answered and never raised my head to look at him.

I guess Mama was embarrassed, because she said, "Molly, where are your manners? Say hello to Mr. Thompson."

My chest hurt so badly. I couldn't move and I couldn't talk. All I could think of was, "Oh my God! What am I going to do? He's found me."

"Dolly, I've missed you," he said. "Are you doing okay?"

Without looking at anyone, I stood up from the table and ran to my room.

That's when I heard Mama tell him, "Don't pay any attention to her, Mr. Thompson. She's just tired."

I shut my door, leaving only a crack open so I could hear what they were saying. I was hoping so bad that Mama would come to my room and see that I was crying. Maybe a red flag would go up and finally she would realize that, just maybe, this was the man who raped me.

"Oh, don't worry about that," I heard Mr. Thompson say. "My daughter's moody like that too. I just stopped by to set up your milk delivery. I don't normally deliver milk to Hendersonville, but for you, I will."

He told her how hard he had tried to find us and told her, "You were always my favorite customer."

I stood behind the door and I waited and I prayed, "Please Mama, make him go away."

I heard her tell him, "You're so nice, Mr. Thompson," and tears filled my eyes.

What was wrong with my mother? She wasn't a dumb woman. She might as well hand me over to him right now, I thought, and I was surprised when she said, "I buy my milk at the grocery store now. It's on my way home from work."

He kept trying to convince her that the milk was better, that it would cost her less, and that it was so easy for him to swing by and put it in the refrigerator. I was sure Mama would give in and sign up for the delivery, but to my surprise and my relief, she never wavered.

Before he left, I heard him say, "If you ever change your mind, just call the company."

And then I heard him say, "Be sure and tell Dolly goodbye for me."

I heard the back door shut and I watched out my bedroom window as he drove away. He was gone, but I knew it wasn't for good. It was at that point that I knew I had to tell somebody. I needed help. I couldn't spend another day in fear, not another day worrying that Mr. Thompson would do to me what Mr. Collier had done to Valerie.

I waited in my room, knowing that any minute Mama would

come in and ask me why I had left the table and was so rude to Mr. Thompson, and I was ready. I was prepared to tell her everything about him, no matter what the result would be, but Mama never came to my room. She didn't even call me back to the table to finish eating supper. Valerie had been raped and murdered in January, and just two years earlier, Dr. B. had told Mama someone had raped me. Sometimes, I think that Mama's mind was going in so many directions and was filled with so much sadness that she had to block some things. It was just more than she could deal with. This time I had thrown the red flag up and gave her every opportunity to find out what was going on with me, but she didn't take it.

Finally I did hear her call my name. She needed help with the dishes, and shortly after the kitchen was clean, she left to go to her night job. My chance had come and gone. If ever I was going to tell her, that was it, and I knew I would never tell her. I had to tell someone, though. If I was going to keep my sanity, I had to tell someone, and the only other person was Paul. He was nineteen years old. He had always been a good big brother to me, and I knew he cared about me. I hoped he would believe me.

Tommy and Paul had gone to the bedroom they shared after supper and were lying on their twin beds when I walked in. The radio was playing and they were talking. Immediately when I walked in, Tommy screamed, "Get out of here."

Tommy was sixteen and didn't seem to like me at all. I wasn't cool enough to be his sister. He acted like he hated my existence. Any other time, I would have left the room when he screamed at me, but this time I didn't care. I had to talk to Paul.

I asked him if he would come out and talk to me, but he didn't want to. I would have to tell him in front of Tommy, but I was determined that I had to do it. It couldn't wait.

I started out by saying, "Mr. Thompson scares me, Paul."

Both of them looked up at me, and Tommy started laughing. He threw his pillow at me and told me I was stupid. "Get out of here," he screamed.

Paul looked at me with concern in his eyes and said, "What are you talking about?"

"He hurt me," I told him. "He grabbed me and he touched me in my private parts and he won't leave me alone."

Tommy laughed again and said, "You have the biggest imagination." And again he screamed at me to get out.

Paul told Tommy to stop and then said, "Tell me what happened."

I proceeded to tell him, "When we lived with Daddy, Mr. Thompson grabbed me and touched me."

I was shaking and choking back the tears, but I was determined not to cry.

For a second, Paul just looked at me and then said, "What are you talking about?" Again Tommy screamed at me, "GET OUT OF HERE!"

I could tell that Paul didn't know what to say or how to respond to what I had just told him. He just looked at me for a few seconds and then said, "I'll talk to you about it later."

He was uncomfortable with the conversation, and if he was going to have it with me, he didn't want to have it in front of Tommy, so I turned and left. I waited patiently in my room all night long, but Paul never came. If anyone was going to help me, I thought it would be him. But for some reason, he must have felt like he couldn't do it. Although he never brought the subject back up to me, I have to think that he believed me but just didn't know what he could possibly do to help me. He also knew, like I did, that if what I was saying was true, it would be too much for Mama to handle. She was working two jobs just to pay the bills and put food on the table. Daddy refused to help her, although the court had ordered him to pay her child support of $125.00 per month. As always, I continued to make excuses for the people I depended on and who I thought could help me.

Later on that night, after my brothers had gone to bed, I wrote Mama a letter. In it I told her all about Mr. Thompson. I told her about the attack and I told her how he had stalked me for the last four years, until we had moved away. I told her how, for that four years, I had hidden under my bed every time he came in, scared to death to even breathe. Now he was back, and I was more frightened than ever. I was afraid that he had come back to kill me. I had to have someone's help, and she was that someone. In the letter, I apologized for bothering her, explaining to her that I knew she had so many more things to worry about. I told her only about Mr. Thompson. I would see how she handled that news before I told her anything else.

Mama worked nights at a nursing home down the street from where we lived. Her shift ended at 7:00 AM, and when she came home, I was waiting for her, the letter in my hand. I hadn't been able to sleep that night. I was unsure how she'd handle what I had written or if she'd even believe me, and I dreaded the outcome.

Mama was so tired when she came in. Work had not gone well, and she was crying. She didn't know how much longer she'd be able to work two jobs. It was getting to be too much for her, and she didn't know how we would live if she had to give the job up. At that instant I felt anger toward Mama, but more than anything I felt pity. I loved her so much. How could I be so insensitive? How could I add more on to her than she already had? As bad as I needed her help, I couldn't dare ask for it. As always, I would handle the situation myself, no matter what the outcome. I tore the letter into tiny pieces and flushed it down the commode.

My confession to Paul and Tommy was never mentioned again— not to me, and not to Mama. I continued to live in fear every day. I watched for Mr. Thompson's truck wherever we went, and I made sure I was never left alone in the house again. He knew where I lived, and I knew he would be back.

After that night, however, I never saw Mr. Thompson again. I continued to see his company trucks around town, but he was never driving them. As time went by, I tried to convince myself that the nightmare was over, but that little voice in my head always assured me that it wasn't. Later in life, after I had told Daddy about Mr. Thompson, I decided to confront Paul about that night. I reminded him of my confession and how he responded when I asked for help. He didn't say much but listened to the things I told him, and when I was finished, this is what he said to me.

"If you knew he was coming, why did you stay in the house? Why didn't you go somewhere away from there until he left?"

"I don't really know," I said. In my room with the door locked and hiding under that bed had become my safe place. He hadn't come through it the first day, and somehow I knew he never would. At least I prayed he wouldn't."

And then I told him, "Besides, Paul, where was I going to go?"

Then he asked me, "Why didn't you tell somebody?"

"I did," I said. "I told you."

I saw the shame cross over his face, and instantly I told him, "It's okay, Paul. You didn't know what to do."

"I'm sorry," was all he could say.

I never blamed Paul for not trying to find out what happened. He wasn't my parent.

When I was sixteen, I started dating Bobby, the man who would become my husband. He was so kind to me and so understanding, and when he finally told me he loved me, I knew he meant it. We dated for eight months before he started pressuring me to have sex, and although I knew he loved me, I knew I'd never let him touch me. It just wouldn't happen, even if it meant losing him.

After a while, however, I grew to love Bobby even more than he loved me, and finally I felt like I had someone in my life whom I could trust, so I told him what had happened to me. I told him about Uncle Tea and about Mr. Thompson and explained why I was so frightened of having sex. Then I asked him, "Why did they hurt me? Why did all of this happen to me?"

It didn't take him but a second to answer. "It's your shyness," he said, "your sweetness, and your innocence. That's what drew me to you."

Bobby was so angry, and more than anything, he was angry at my family for letting it happen. He threatened to go find Mr. Thompson, but I begged him not to. "I'll find him," he said, "and when I'm through with him, you'll never have to worry about him again."

I started crying and told him, "If he knows I told on him, he'll kill me for sure. Please don't go there." He said he wouldn't, but he didn't promise.

A few weeks had passed and we were out on a date one night when abruptly he said, "Molly, I found Mr. Thompson, and he can't hurt you anymore."

"Oh my God," I screamed. "What have you done?"

"Listen to me," he answered. "He can't hurt you anymore because he's dead. He died last year."

I choked back the tears and told him, "You're just saying that."

"No," he said, "it's the truth. He can't hurt you anymore. He's dead."

And then he said, "I'll take you there. I'll take you to his grave. I'll show you where he's buried. Then you can let it go."

I became so emotional. "Don't you understand?" I told him. "The man has terrorized me since I was ten years old. For six years, I've been in fear for my life every day and every night. How can I ever let it go?" I sobbed so hard that I could hardly talk.

When I finally realized that Bobby was telling me the truth, I told him, "I don't want to see his grave. I have to trust that you're telling me the truth."

"You can trust me," he said. "I wouldn't lie to you." Then he told me that he knew where his wife and children lived. He had two sons and a daughter, just as Mr. Thompson had said. They were a rich, prominent family in the town where they lived. He told me he would take me to see them and I could tell them what he did to me.

Mr. Thompson's family didn't hurt me; he did. In my mind, I wanted to believe that he was a good husband and a good father and for some reason, he did something that he would never have done and then he didn't know how to stop it. I didn't want to hurt his family. If what Bobby said was true, then he couldn't hurt me anymore. In the back of my mind, too, I prayed that he hadn't hurt anyone else on his milk route. If he did, I have no one to blame but myself.

Many years later, when I was diagnosed with bipolar illness, along with seeing a psychiatrist on a regular basis, I was assigned a case worker. She came to the house every month to see me, and we developed a friendship. I talked to her about some of the things that had happened to me, including Mr. Thompson. It turned out that she lived in the same hometown as he did, and just as Bobby had told me, his family was well known. I told her about his attack and how he stalked me for four more years. I told her how I hid under my bed every time he came, drawn up in a fetal position, sucking my thumb and praying that he would go away. She was shocked. She couldn't imagine him ever doing something like that. She said he was well respected in town and had a beautiful family. She told me that if people had found out what he did, it would have ruined him. She also told me that he had died many years ago, just as Bobby had said. Then she told me something that I couldn't believe was true.

She told me that Mr. Thompson had come down with a rare illness for which he was bedridden, and when he died, he was drawn up in a fetal position and was sucking his thumb. She said that because his family was so well known everyone in town knew it.

Although she could tell I didn't believe her, she insisted that it was true. I had prayed that Mr. Thompson would die, but I wouldn't have wished that kind of death on him. He had made my life hell. I was like a scared animal, always being stalked, fearful that at any minute I'd be caught and my life would be over.

All I really wanted to know was that he was dead and couldn't hurt me or anybody else ever again. But the pain he instilled upon me has been lifelong. I wish I could forget it, but I can't.

EARS

I was fifteen years old and a freshman in high school when I was asked out on my first date. A girl's first date should be one of the most exciting and the most anticipated times in her life and it should have been that for me. But it wasn't. I started dreading it years before it might happen, and I actually never expected it to happen. When it did, it turned out badly. As with most of my experiences, I was caught off guard and didn't know how to handle myself, but for the first time in my life, I wasn't the one who was hurt. I hurt somebody else, and it couldn't be undone.

It was my first year away from St. John's. I had been with the same children for the five past years and also under the strict, dominant rule of the nuns. St. John's had felt like a prison, and although I felt freedom in the public school that I had never known, I was terrified of my new environment and the prospect of having to make new friends.

I met Ears the first day of school in study hall. His name was David, but he had been tagged with the nickname "Ears" because his ears stuck straight out from his head. He was tall and lanky, about six feet tall, and had brown hair that looked as though it was never combed. His teeth were scraggly, of every shape and size, and so his outer appearance wasn't attractive. But as soon as he started talking and spread that huge grin across his face, he was absolutely adorable. Everyone in school knew him and liked him, and it's easy to say that he was probably the most popular boy in the sophomore class.

It was during that hour in study hall that my freshman friends and Ears' sophomore friends came to know each other. I was the shy girl who didn't talk much. At St. John's, the nuns had insisted that we speak only when spoken to, and so rarely did I contribute to any conversation unless I had something to say that I felt was worth saying. Everyone started calling me the "chatterbox." I didn't like it. All it meant to me was that I had no personality. It seemed that the one thing, the only thing, I had going for me was that I was nice, especially nice, to everyone, and that seemed to get me by.

After class one day, Ears walked me to my locker, and even though I felt comfortable with him, I still didn't talk to him much. That's why I was completely surprised when my friends informed me that he was going to ask me out. I liked the attention Ears gave me, but I had already decided that that's as far as it would go. There was no way I would go on a date with him or with anybody else, for that matter, so I started avoiding him in every way possible. Every day I would move to a different seat in study hall, but it didn't matter where I sat, Ears made sure that he sat close to me.

Finally, one Friday, when school was just about to let out, Ears came up behind me at my locker. He put his arms around me and whispered in my ear. "Guess what?" he said, "It's been approved. You're going to be my girl." I froze. I couldn't believe he was touching me, and once again that familiar sense of panic came over me and I couldn't breathe. I wanted to struggle and free myself from him and run, and if there hadn't been so many people walking in the hall, I would have.

When I didn't answer him, he whispered in my ear again, "My friends think we're a good match. Do you want to be my girl?" Still I stood speechless. My throat tightened up, and as hard as I could, I tried not to cry. What I wanted to do was scream at him as loud as I could, "Why are you touching me? Take your hands off me!" But instead I stood still and silent. I didn't want to embarrass myself or him.

That's when Ears stepped around in front of me and leaned down into my face. For an instant I thought he was going to kiss me, and I was horrified. It had been a long time since I had let anyone get that close to me. Before I could move or say anything, he put his hand on my chin and raised my face to look at him, and as sweetly as anyone had ever spoken to me, he looked me in the eyes and said, "Will you go on a date with me this weekend?"

I didn't give him enough time to tell me what night he wanted the date or what he had planned. My instant response was, "I'm sorry. I can't," and I jerked away from him, but he wouldn't give up.

"Why not?" he said. "Don't you want to go out with me?"

I turned away from him and pressed my body up against the locker. "It's not you," I said. "My mother won't let me date yet." And I hoped that would be the end of it.

"Is that all?" he said, "Tommy likes me. He'll talk your mom into it." I felt bad for Ears. It was almost as though he was begging. Any girl in school would feel lucky that he asked her out, so why did he want to go out with me? I was nobody. I was so shy that I couldn't even carry on a conversation with him. I didn't want to hurt Ears' feelings, and never would I intentionally do that, but he was giving me no choice. I didn't answer him and I didn't look at him, and finally he turned and started to walk away, but not before he said, "I'll talk to Tommy. He'll fix it."

Ears was bound and determined, but then so was I. It wouldn't matter what Tommy said to Mama; I was not going on a date, not with Ears, not with anybody.

Paul had turned sixteen and had started dating when I was ten years old. On a daily basis, I had listened to Mama rant and rave at him, "Don't you do things you shouldn't do! Nice girls won't let you touch them! No man will ever want to marry a girl who has been damaged!"

Then Tommy had turned sixteen and started dating, and it was the same thing all over again. The accusations never stopped. As far as I know, she had never sat down with either of them and had the talk about girls and dating and sex. She made everything seem nasty and horrible, and it made me feel as though my brothers were bad and were doing horrible things to girls, the same horrible things that had been done to me.

It took a while for everything she was saying to make sense, but finally it became clear to me. I was the girl she was talking about. I was the girl who was "damaged," and if what she was saying was true, then no man would ever want to marry me, and Mama knew that. That's why she had kept my rape a secret.

I had listened to Mama fuss at my brothers for several years before my time to date came, and so when Ears asked me out, I knew I couldn't go. I was scared to death at the thought of being alone with him. All of my friends had already started dating. They were so happy and excited about life, and I wished so hard that I could be like them, but I had already resigned myself to the fact that I would never have the life my friends would have. I wasn't worthy.

When I got home from school that afternoon, I didn't mention anything about Ears to Mama. I didn't have time. Tommy had already beat me to it.

"Molly got asked out on a date today," he told Mama, laughing about it, and then he asked me, "Why did you tell Ears 'no'?"

I didn't answer him calmly. I screamed at him, "Because I don't want to and no one can make me!"

It caught both him and Mama off guard. He proceeded to tell Mama about Ears, what a good guy he was, and that she should make me go out with him.

I was furious and screamed again, "Mind you own business! I'm not going!"

"I don't know why he would want to go out with you anyway," he screamed back. "You're a loser!"

That's when Mama chimed in, "Do you like him?"

Of course the only answer I could give her was "yes."

"Then why don't you want to go?" she asked.

She had to know why not. Why was she acting so dumb? That's exactly the question I wanted to ask her.

Instead I screamed at her too, "I'm not going and you can't make me!"

The only other time I could ever remember raising my voice at Mama was when she made me go to Valerie's funeral and I had told her then that never again would she make me do something I didn't want to do. After that night at the funeral home, I had started having periods of outbursts. Mostly they were aimed at Tommy. He was a normal teenage brother who hated his little sister, and it had gotten harder and harder to take his constant teasing and criticism. Mama thought he was the reason for my behavior.

After I screamed at her, Mama and I stood silent, staring at each other. I halfway hoped that she'd scream back at me and that an all-out battle would ensue, but she just looked at me and I saw something in her eyes that I had never seen before. It was pity. She understood. She knew why I was refusing to go.

It was at that second when I hoped she would take me aside, away from Tommy, and explain things to me. I wanted her to tell me that what happened wasn't my fault and I wasn't "damaged goods." I wanted her to hug me and tell me she loved me and that whatever decision I made was okay with her. I hoped we'd have the mother-daughter talk. I wanted her to tell what to expect the date to be like and how to handle myself if an uncomfortable situation arose, and for a second I stood there and waited for her to offer some sort of encouragement and advice, but I got nothing. I even hoped that she'd start fussing at me and warn me about having sex, just like she always did with Paul and Tommy. I would have been glad just to have that conversation with her, but she dropped the subject.

All I knew to expect from any man was what they had done to me, and the thought of going through it again was more than I could imagine. I was afraid that the next time it happened, I might not be able to save myself. It was unimaginable that Ears would ever hurt me; but if he tried, what would I do? Finally I told myself that whatever happened, I would handle it, just as I always had.

"I'll go, Mama," I told her calmly, "if that's what you want me to do."

She smiled and said, "Yes, you go and have a good time."

Not that day or any day after did she ever have the talk with me. As usual, I was left to fend for myself.

All afternoon and into the night, I dreaded hearing the phone ring. I tried to tell myself that Ears had changed his mind and wouldn't call, but finally he did. He was so happy when I told him I would go. His plans were to double-date on Saturday night with his best friend, Phillip, and his girlfriend, Kay. The plan was to go to Shoney's to eat and then to the drive-in movie, and I felt sick. Mama and I had been to the drive-in movie before and I had seen the teenagers in the cars next to us. First you could see them smothering each other with kisses, and then you couldn't see them at all, not until the movie was over. I didn't have to use my imagination to know what they were doing.

As soon as Ears mentioned the drive-in movie, I started thinking of some way to get out of going, but nothing would come to mind. The only thing that might save me would be the couple going with us. Surely I would be safe. Surely Ears wouldn't try anything if they were with us.

I didn't sleep at all that night. The next day I was a bundle of nerves. I tried to isolate myself from Mama and my brothers, but our house was so small that there was nowhere to hide. My brothers teased me all day about Ears and the upcoming date. "What will you do when he kisses you?" they teased. They didn't say "if he kisses you" but "when he kisses you," so it was a given that I would be faced with that. The idea that it might happen was funny to them. They had no idea what it was doing to me. I was terrified.

All day long, Mr. Thompson kept coming to mind. It had been only a few months since he had re-appeared at our back door. I thought back about that night when I told Paul and Tommy that he had attacked me. At the time, my brothers didn't believe me. They had laughed at me. What was it going to take for my family to see what was happening to me? At any minute I was going to explode. Is that what it would take for them to believe me? Did I have to have a total breakdown?

The more the teasing went on the more I wanted to scream, "Do you want to know why I don't want to go? This is why!" and I would tell them everything. Before they could interrupt me, before they could laugh at me, before they could call me an idiot, I would tell everything. They would have no choice but to listen. That little voice in the back of my head always stopped me.

Ears was supposed to pick me up a 6:30 PM, and he was right on time. My nerves were shot. I waited in my room, watching out the window, and stayed there as long as I could before Mama had to come drag me out. Shyly, I grinned at Ears and introduced him to Mama. As we walked to the car, I saw that he had already picked Phillip up, but not Kay. I was going to be alone with them, both of them! How would I ever defend myself?

I was forced to sit in the front seat in the middle of Ears and Phillip, and during the drive to Kay's house, they talked and they laughed and I never said a word. I sat frozen, trying not to rub up against either one of them, so scared that they would feel my body shaking. Once we picked Kay up, some sense of relief came over me and the night started out okay.

Shoney's was the local drive-in restaurant that everyone hung out at, and until we could find a parking spot, we drove round and round and round. The boys normally got out of the cars and gathered in groups to talk, which is what Phillip did, but Ears stayed in the car with me. We ordered our food, and for more than an hour, we sat, we talked, and we listened to music playing over the intercom. I felt so stupid. Why had I dreaded being with him so much? Ears made me feel as though there was nobody else around but him and me, and as I sat there, I thought it was probably the best time I had ever had in my life and I didn't want it to end. Once again I let my guard down.

After we ate, we left the restaurant, but Ears didn't turn in the direction of the drive-in theater. Instead he drove straight to the Old Hickory Dam, the favorite parking spot for teenagers. It had barely turned dark, and already there were half-a-dozen cars parked there. As soon as Ears stopped our car, I could hear Phillip and Kay kissing. Almost immediately, they lay down in the back seat and went at it. Before I knew it, Ears had moved over so close to me that I couldn't move. My body was pressed tight against the door. He wrapped his arms around me and without saying a word started kissing my neck. I can't even explain the horror that came over me. I stiffened up and closed my eyes and screamed inside myself, "Stop. Oh God. Please stop!"

I felt like I was being attacked all over again, and I knew I couldn't let it happen. I started feeling for the doorknob, and in an instant the car door was open and I was out of the car. I gave no thought to where I was going. I just knew I had to get away, and I started running as fast as I could. Before I knew it, Ears had gotten hold of me and I was fighting him. All he was trying to do was calm me down, but I didn't really realize that it was him. I was fighting my attacker. I didn't know where I was, who I was with, or what I was doing there, and it was only when Ears started talking to me that I realized what I was doing. I had gone crazy.

Finally I realized that it was Ears who had his arms around me and

I calmed down. When he asked me what was wrong, all I could tell him was that I was sick and needed to go home. He kept apologizing and asking me if he hurt me, and I tried to reassure him that he didn't. I was so humiliated. It was the first time in my life that I was unable to control my fear.

Ears was so sweet. He took my hand and walked with me back to the car. Phillip and Kay were sitting up watching everything that was going on. As soon as we got back into the car, Phillip wanted to know what was going on and Ears told him, "She doesn't feel good. I'm taking her home." Not another word was spoken, not by anyone. I never looked at Ears on the drive home. I stared out the window and wished I was dead.

When we drove into my driveway, he hardly had time to put the car in park before I flung the door open and ran toward the front door. Ears was right behind me, and before I could open the front door, he grabbed my arm and stopped me. Again he said, "Molly, tell me what I did. I didn't mean to hurt you."

I was so ashamed. I couldn't look him in the eyes. "You didn't hurt me, Ears. I told you I'm sick. I never should have gone out tonight."

Without saying anything else to me, Ears turned and walked back to his car. I stood at the front door and watched him, so embarrassed and so humiliated, not for myself but for him.

Mama was asleep in her rocking chair. Tommy and Paul weren't home yet. As quietly as I could, I crept to my bedroom, shut the door, and broke down. I closed my eyes, pulled my hair, and screamed inside myself. I cursed Mama, I cursed Tommy, and I cursed myself. Something was wrong with me. I wasn't normal. I was crazy. Why did it have to be in front Ears and his friends that I finally showed my true self?

I didn't sleep a wink that night. My body wouldn't be still. It was as though a million ants were crawling through me.

The next morning at breakfast, Mama asked me if I had a good time and what movie I saw. I told her I got sick after we ate and had to come home. I didn't dare tell her about the Old Hickory Dam and what I had done.

Ears was the first boy who had ever shown me any attention, the first boy who was ever nice to me. Now he would hate me. Everyone would hate me. Exactly what I didn't want to happen had happened, but I wasn't the one hurt this time. I had hurt someone else, and there was no way to undo what I had done.

Monday rolled around and I dreaded going to school. Foolishly, I hoped that no one knew what I had done, but just as I suspected, everyone knew. The day was miserable. Ears was teased to death, but he just laughed it off. I was asked a million questions and branded as an "idiot," and rightly so. I didn't expect Ears ever to speak to me again and was totally surprised when he took his same seat beside me in study hall. It was hard for me to look at him or talk to him, but he continued to walk me to my locker after every class and called me every night. He acted as though nothing had happened. When the weekend came, he asked me out on a date and I told him, "No." Finally, after several weeks, Ears gave up on me. He stopped calling and spoke to me only when he had to. My friends told me I was a "fool," but I already knew that.

Summer finally rolled around and school let out and I didn't see Ears anymore. I talked with my friends on the phone, I went to slumber parties and watched them date while I sat home alone, but I didn't mind. It seemed that loneliness was my destiny.

One night late that summer, Paul came home from being out with his friends. He had unimaginable news, which he directed straight at me. "Your boyfriend, Ears, was in a wreck a while ago," he said. "I just helped scoop his body parts up off the highway."

I waited for him to grin and say he was just joking, but I knew Paul wouldn't joke about something like that. He proceeded to tell Tommy what he knew about the accident and all of the gory details. Ears was driving down a four-lane highway. He was speeding. He crossed over the center line and hit another car head on. Two of his best friends were in the car with him. All three of them were killed. Ears was dead. He was just sixteen years old.

When I started crying, Tommy came out with something so hurtful that I've never forgotten it. "Why are you crying?" he said. "You didn't even like Ears."

"Shut up," I screamed back at him. "You don't know anything about it."

"Yeah, I do," he said. "I know all about it. I know what you did." Tommy had never asked me about my date with Ears, and stupidly I thought that no one would tell him, but he had known the whole time. I wondered why he had never said anything to me. And why did he have to say it now? Why did he have to be so cruel? I was crazy about Ears, but I had never let him or anyone else know it. He was dead and I couldn't make things right. It was too late.

When Mama heard what Tommy said, she asked him what he was talking about. "Ask her," he said.

Before she could ask me anything, I ran out the front door. I didn't dare tell Mama what happened, and I didn't want to be there when Tommy did. For quite a while, I walked the streets of my neighborhood and cried. I talked to myself and I talked to Ears. I tried to explain things to him, and I told him how sorry I was. Like so many times before, I felt like I was going crazy. I wanted to scream at the top of my lungs. What had happened with Ears was the first sign. I was having a total breakdown. I could feel it. Ears' death was just the thing to push me over the edge. I couldn't hide inside myself anymore.

As I walked back home, I prepared myself for the questions Mama would ask me. Paul and Tommy would be there too, all of them waiting for me to explain myself, but by the time I got home, everyone had scattered. Paul and Tommy had left the house, and Mama seemed to busy herself when I came in. I could tell she didn't want to talk to me. If she was concerned about what happened with Ears, she never asked me and I never offered an explanation. The subject was never mentioned.

For days, all everyone talked about were the upcoming funerals, and for days I didn't sleep. I couldn't stop thinking about what Paul had said, "I scooped his body parts up off the highway." Whenever I tried to close my eyes, I saw myself standing at Ears' casket looking down at him, and all that was there were body parts and I was screaming, "I'm sorry! I'm sorry!" I kept thinking about Valerie and the huge hole in her head. If they couldn't fix it, how would they ever fix Ears?

The day of the funeral came. The plan was to meet my best friend there, but at the last minute, I called and told her I wasn't going. "Ears really liked you, Molly," she said in anger. "How can you not go?"

My voice trembled and I strained to get the words out without breaking down. "I just can't go," I told her. I offered no other excuse.

That afternoon, while the funeral was taking place, I stayed home alone. Tommy had gone to the funeral, and Mama and Paul had gone to work. For two hours, I paced from one end of the house to the other trying to convince myself that I was right for not going. I told myself that I would have made a complete spectacle of myself, just as I had at Valerie's funeral. I told myself that Ears deserved respect. He didn't deserve any more humiliation, not from me. But no matter how much I talked to myself, no matter what reason I gave, it was wrong of me not to go.

Finally Tommy returned home from the funeral. He had never seen so many people waiting to pay their respects to the families. Ears' casket was closed. His body was in too bad a shape to be shown. Just as I suspected, they weren't able to fix him.

For weeks after his death, I couldn't get visions of the accident and the descriptions Paul had given out of my head. I didn't call my friends or accept calls from them either. The shame of what I had done overwhelmed me and I isolated myself from everything and everybody. I became more and more rebellious. All my family had to do was look at me the wrong way and I attacked. It had gotten pretty bad after Valerie's murder, but after Ears died, something just snapped and I could no longer control my anger. Every time I opened my mouth, I sassed Mama. It didn't do any good for her to ground me. What could she ground me from?

Since I was five years old, I had done everything I could to protect myself because there was no one else to protect me, and I had struggled really hard to keep my sanity. I don't know whether it was turning fifteen and maturity that took over or if it was the death of my two close friends that finally sent me over the edge. But I was determined that nobody would ever hurt me again. I would fight like hell if they tried.

MY FIRST LOVE

That summer, after my freshman year, Mama got restless once again and decided that we would move back home, to the Cracker Jack box. We had lived in Hendersonville for one year so that Tommy could get established in school and on the football team. Now that he was, it was time to go home. I could not have been happier. I had made some good friends there, but Gallatin was my home and I was ready to go.

That summer, I became acquainted with my old friends again and made new friends; it was the best summer ever. We went to the swimming pool every day, we had slumber parties, and we went to dances on the weekend. I didn't remember being that happy since we left the farm. I made my mind up to put all my bad memories behind me. There was nothing I could do to change the past, but this was my chance for a new start, and I wouldn't let anything or anybody spoil it.

At the slumber parties, dating and sex seemed to be the major topic of discussion, and although I already knew about most things involving sex, I went out of my way to play dumb. When the other girls talked about sex, I never got into the conversation. I acted like I didn't know anything. My excuse was that I came from the Catholic school and sex was never discussed. When they laughed at me, I would say to myself, "If you only knew what I knew, you wouldn't be laughing." I wasn't the dumb one. They were, and no matter how much they teased me, I never gave myself away. I did all I could do to prevent them from knowing about me. When my friends started dating, I didn't. I was rarely asked, but when I was, I always gave an excuse. Never would I put myself in that position again.

When school started in the fall, it was great. I had all my friends around me, and the best thing about it was that Tommy was in a different school. I was sick of him making fun of me in front of his friends and teasing me. More than anyone in my life, he was the one who had made me feel embarrassed and inferior to other people. On the weekends, I had to endure his criticism and teasing, but I had gotten better about handling him. We always ended up screaming at each other, but most of the time I was able to stand my ground. The main thing about going to different schools was that I felt like my friends liked me for me, not because Tommy was my brother.

School started in the fall and I was a sophomore, and although I had lots of friends around me, I always felt lonely. I felt like the oddball. I wanted to feel the same happiness and excitement my friends felt, but it didn't seem to be in my reach. I still refused to let anyone get close to me. My past wouldn't release me.

In January of the next year, right before my sixteenth birthday, my brother Paul brought one of his friends home with him. His name was Bobby. I liked him from the start. My brothers brought a lot of friends home with them, but none of them ever paid any attention to me; why he did, I still don't know. For the first time in my life I felt comfortable talking to someone of the opposite sex, and I found myself feeling something I had never felt. I wanted him to ask me out. I wanted to spend time with him, away from Mama, away from my brothers, but he was twenty-three years old, seven years older than me. I was just a kid compared to him. There's no way it would ever happen, and I didn't dare wish for it. Everything in my past told me that if it happened, it would only turn out badly.

That's why I was totally surprised when he asked me to go sledding one snowy night with Paul and his date. Although I still felt shy around him, Bobby had a way of bringing me out of my shell. Unlike my date with Ears, I felt like I was ready to date, and I felt comfortable being with Bobby. Never did I feel that he would do anything that might bother me. When we were done sledding, we sat around a bonfire, and although most of the couples were huddled up and were kissing, Bobby never put his hands on me and never tried to kiss me, and although I felt a huge sense of relief, I also wished he had. I didn't want the night to end.

The next day it snowed again, and that night Paul and Bobby went sledding again. But Bobby didn't ask me to go. He asked Joyce, one of my friends, to go. She was pretty and bubbly and full of personality. I knew he would have more fun, but I was devastated and spent the whole night in my room crying. As usual, I didn't dare let Mama see me. I was still intent on not letting anyone see my true feelings, and I couldn't shake it.

The next night, Bobby came to the house to pick Paul up to go sledding again. When he came in, I didn't speak to him, and when I felt the familiar tightening in my throat and the tears welling up, I went to my room and hid. I wasn't mad at Bobby. I didn't blame him for asking Joyce. He had to have had more fun with her. I knew I hadn't talked much the night before. It wasn't that I was just shy. I was scared of saying the wrong thing and sounding dumb. In fact, I was quite boring and I knew it. Once again I resigned myself to the fact that the things other girls had just wasn't meant for me. I had to quit wishing for it to happen.

Only a minute had passed when Mama came to my room and told me that Bobby wanted to talk to me. When I walked into the room, he put his hand out and said, "Come on; let's go sledding." My heart felt like it would jump out of my chest. I tried not to look him in the eyes. I didn't want him to see that I was about to cry. Bobby kissed me that night and held me, and for the first time, I wasn't afraid of a man touching me. It was my first kiss, and I was in love. God had finally smiled down upon me.

Bobby and I were never apart again. We dated through high school and into college, and after five years we got married. I told him every secret I had, and he did all he could to make me feel safe and happy. When I think back about Bobby, it's as though, instinctively, he knew that he had to handle me with kid gloves. It was as though he needed someone to take care of. He did that night and the rest of my life, and I thanked God many times for bringing him to me.

I am reminded of a quote that describes perfectly the way I felt about Bobby then and the way I still feel:

"Too often we underestimate the power of a touch, a smile, a kind word, a listening ear, an honest compliment or the smallest act of caring, all of which have the potential to turn a life around."

---Leo Buscaglia

WHERE ARE THE
GOOD MEMORIES?

The journals I wrote for Dr. J. were about things that happened to me from the age of five until I was fifteen years old, but they were about the bad memories only. I had not written down one good memory about my childhood, with the exception of the memories I have of my grandmother, Mammie. She was probably the only adult in my life when I was a child who made me feel really loved and even after I grew into adulthood, she was always there for me. We would spend hours sitting out on her front porch talking to each other and laughing. I could tell her anything and knew it would never be repeated. But as much as I loved her and trusted her, I never confided in her the experiences I went through and I don't why. I have to think it's because of what Uncle Tea said: "If they find out what you did, they won't love you anymore."

My good memories are very few and far between, but there are some. The very first Barbie doll came out in 1959. I was eight years old. It was the same year that Kathy died and the same year that Mama and Daddy divorced. I wanted the doll so much, but knew better than to ask for it. All I could do was hope that Santa would bring it to me for Christmas, but he didn't. The doll cost $3.00, but Mama had a hard time just putting food on the table; at least that's what she told us on a daily basis.

The Christmas of 1960, Santa finally brought her to me. I don't remember ever being more excited in my life than when I held that doll in my hands. She came with a small round case, and in it were clothes that Mama had knitted and sewn for her. She had also made Barbie a canopy bed out of a shoe box and empty spools of thread. The bedspread, pillow, and canopy cover were made of white eyelet. Somehow, Mama had managed to make all if it without me knowing it.

Barbie became more than just a doll to me. She was my best friend. I talked to her as though she was human and held her in my arms when I felt lonely and afraid. All these years later, I still have her and all the clothes Mama made her. The bed eventually tore up and was thrown away. Not before Kathy or since Kathy's death had I loved anything more than my Barbie doll.

One of my other good memories, and the only good memory I have of my time at St. John's, was when I was in the seventh grade. A contest was going on. We were selling candy and the child who sold the most won an eight-by-ten picture of Mary, the Blessed Virgin. Because we were taught in school to fear God for the simple sins we committed, I turned to Mary for help when I prayed. She was a woman and a mother, and it seemed that she'd understand my prayers more than God. I would kneel beneath her statue on the altar in church and I would light a candle; even if my prayers weren't answered, somehow I knew she was listening.

Along with winning the picture of Mary, the child who won would place a crown of flowers on Mary's head at the Mother of May celebration. For weeks, I went from door to door and, as shy as I was, begged people to buy the candy from me. I still don't know how I did it, but I won. I never felt so much pride in myself, but along with that pride, I felt that I was not worthy of placing the crown on Her head. I was not one of the more popular children in school, so I felt like everyone was disappointed when I won. Before I climbed the ladder that day to place the crown on Mary's head, I looked back at the faces of the other children standing below. I didn't know whether the disappointment I saw on their faces was because I won the honor or because they themselves had not won. I told myself that I won because Mary wanted me to. That picture hung over my bed for years, and when I got down on my knees at night, I looked at the picture when I prayed. It's one of the only things I saved from my childhood, other than my Barbie doll.

As hard as I've tried, I can't think of any other good things that happened in my life. Everything about our lives seemed to be gloom and doom. Mama cried all the time because of money problems. Once she had to sell our dining room table and chairs so she could buy groceries. Daddy wouldn't help us, and so we lived from day to day, not knowing what tomorrow would bring. The only things that ever seemed to make Mama happy were things that involved Tommy. Throughout my journals, I didn't have too many good things to say about him, but Tommy and I were close in age, which made it hard to get along. Paul was six years older than me. Our relationship was more like that of an adult and child. He cared about me and I knew it. Even today, as grown adults, Paul always hugs me when he sees me and never fails to tell me he loves me. Tommy would rather be shot, but I do know, in my heart, that if I needed him, he would be there for me.

Paul and Tommy were both involved in sports. While Paul only played football, Tommy played football, baseball, and basketball. Anytime he needed uniforms and shoes, somehow Mama found the money for them. I remember wanting to take dance lessons, but I refused to when Mama bought used shoes and outfits from the other mothers. I wanted new things just like the other girls. I didn't pitch a fit about it though. I just accepted the fact that it was something I couldn't do.

I was a child who never expected anything good to happen to me, and when it did, I always felt like I was unworthy. My inferiority complex took over my life. Although I know that the reason was because of everything that had happened to me, there were so many other reasons too. I was always hesitant to look anybody in the eyes for fear they would know about me, so most of the time I didn't talk. I just watched and listened and wished I was like the other children.

Other than the bad experiences, there were other things that really bothered me. I didn't have a daddy. At least, I felt like I didn't. I was embarrassed that my parents were divorced. Birthdays and Christmas always came and went and I would never hear from him. I hated where I lived, I didn't have my own room, and didn't want my friends to see my house. I would spend the night with other girls, but not once did I ever invite them to my house, and Mama never encouraged it.

One of the things my daughters were always allowed to do was completely decorate their own rooms, pick out paint colors, curtains, and bedspreads, and hang posters on the walls. It was an important experience for them. I think it played a big part in developing their characters. They also had a place they could call their own, a place to invite their friends to, a place where they could share ideas and opinions. They could talk about all the silly things that girls talk about. That in itself probably helped them develop friendships with their peers.

Mine and Mama's bedroom was extremely small. It was always painted a dull beige color. There was nothing hanging on the walls. There were no pretty knickknacks placed around. We shared the closet and the dresser. All it was was a place to sleep. I don't really know the right words to use here, but it's as though I never had the chance to develop a relationship with myself. All children need that.

It was not until I turned seventeen that I finally had a room of my own. That happened when Mama got remarried. I had my own room for one year before I went off to college, and for that little time I enjoyed it more than most girls could even think about.

As parents, we hope that we make the lives of our children memorable ones, and we hope that the good times outweigh the bad. But there are going to be bad times in their lives and all we can hope for is that they trust us and give us a chance to help them through those times.

MARGARET

I have three daughters, Elizabeth, Margaret and Kathryn. I started talking to them about sex when they were ten years old. I wanted to do it when they were five, but I didn't think they were old enough to understand. When I had the talk, I left nothing out. I explained the monthly period to them, I explained female and male body parts, and I told them about bad people that could hurt them. I wanted them to be prepared for anything that could possibly happen.

In 1975, when my first daughter was three years old, a little girl who lived in Nashville went missing while she was going from door to door selling Girl Scout cookies. Her name was Marcia Trimble. From the moment I heard about her on TV, I became obsessed with her. I worried so much about her that it made me physically sick, and when they didn't find her that first night, I knew she was dead. Over the years, I had tried my best not to think about Uncle Tea and Mr. Thompson, although they were always in the back of my mind. I tried to center my attention solely on keeping my daughters safe, but when Marcia went missing, everything came back into my mind and I felt like it had happened just yesterday. I couldn't rest. I knew what had been done to her, and I actually felt the fear she must have known when she was being attacked. They found her body thirty-three days later in a garage. She had been raped and murdered. She was just nine years old.

All I could think of was "Where were her parents? Why did they let this happen?" I was already obsessed with keeping my daughter safe, and after Marcia was murdered, I could think of nothing else. Because of everything that happened to me, I made it hard on all my daughters when they were growing up. I was a constant watchdog, scared to death to let them out of my sight. When they became old enough to date, it was even worse. But as I said before, no matter how good a parent you try to be, there are things that are just out of your control.

My second daughter, Margaret, was born with Williams Syndrome. It's a rare condition occurring in approximately 1 to 20,000 live births. *The Williams Syndrome Foundation* describes the condition as: "a genetically determined, intellectually disabling condition. A micro deletion on chromosome 7 has been identified in affected individuals and individuals with WS are often of short stature, slight build and also appear to age prematurely. The condition is characterized by mild to moderate intellectual disability or learning problems, unique personality characteristics, distinctive facial features and heart and blood vessel (cardiovascular) problems."

In *The New York Times* there was a recent article titled *The Gregarious Brain* that really describes my daughter. It reads that "a person with Williams Syndrome will live not only with some fairly conventional cognitive deficits but also a strange set of traits that researchers call the "Williams personality": a love of company and conversation combined, often awkwardly, with a poor understanding of social dynamics and a lack of social inhibition. They may approach strangers in an over-friendly and over-familiar manner. This can be a major worry for parents and carers, who fear that they are too trusting and could be taken advantage of if not supervised sufficiently."

Although Margaret is thirty-four years old now, she seems to have the mentality of a thirteen or fourteen year old. She is extremely friendly and makes conversation with everyone she sees. She never forgets a face or the name that goes with it. Our major concern with Margaret has always been her over-friendliness and her trusting nature.

I never suspected that anything was wrong with Margaret until her daycare teacher suggested I have her tested. There were very few signs. I knew that she couldn't swing on a swing set because she would panic and start screaming and she couldn't walk up or down a staircase. She crawled. But I contributed both of those problems to her eyes. Since birth, her right eye stayed inward at her nose and the optometrist said the muscles were not fully developed so he prescribed glasses for her. It didn't solve those particular problems but I still never suspected that anything else could be wrong.

She was just three years old when we took her to Vanderbilt Hospital for testing. At first, they thought she had autism but the final diagnosis was Williams Syndrome. Before they could even explain to me what the syndrome was, I completely broke down. This couldn't be happening to my child. Why my child? Even after they explained it to me, I still couldn't see it or maybe I didn't want to.

Everyone kept telling me, "God won't put more on you than he thinks you can bear," and then they'd say, "He only gives special children to special people." I didn't want to hear it. My child would never have the life I hoped for her. She would face difficult challenges every day, and more than anything, I knew how lonely her life would be. People are not very accepting of things they don't understand, especially children.

As she began to get older, Margaret's life did get harder, but I thanked God every day for giving her to me. I loved all three of my daughters, but Margaret needed me more than the others, and the amount of love she gave me in return was more than I could ever imagine receiving from anyone. Because she was with me so much, it wasn't hard to keep her safe. If I wasn't with her, I knew her dad or sisters would be. Everyone was protective of her. There was no way anyone could hurt her but I let my guard down and took her safety for granted.

I was working at a law firm in Nashville when it happened. Margaret was eighteen years old. I received a call from my husband one day at work and was told to come home. Something had happened to her. Although I begged him to tell me what, he wouldn't. "Just come home," he said. I didn't know if she was alive or dead, and I cried all the way home. When I got there, her daddy, her sisters, and her grandmother were hovering around her. She was in hysterics. She had been raped.

When my husband told me, I thought my head was going to explode. I wanted to scream at the top of my lungs. How could this have happened? How? I didn't scream, however. I had to stay calm. I knew it would be the only way she would confide in me. I took her upstairs to her room, away from everyone else, and asked her to tell me what happened.

She told me that a boy had been calling her on the telephone for quite a while. Only he wasn't a boy; he was a man. She had never seen him or met him, but she thought that someone liked her. That's all she cared about. She wanted a boyfriend, just like her sisters had. The man's name was Kenneth. That day, Kenneth had called and asked her to go riding with him. He told her he didn't want to come to the house. He wasn't ready to meet her parents. He talked her into walking down the street where he would pick her up. She told me that as soon as she saw him, she knew who he was and became frightened. Still he was able to talk her into his truck. He drove a couple of miles out into the country, parked behind a barn, and raped her. He also made her perform oral sex on him.

Inside, I felt like I was losing it, but I couldn't let Margaret see that. The main reason I had never told Mama about the attacks on me was because I didn't want to upset her. I knew I had to be strong for my daughter, and I had to make her know that, no matter what, what happened was not her fault.

Margaret went on to tell me that when Kenneth drove her home, he let her out at the driveway and told her to go into the garage, take her clothes off, and come back out naked, where he could see her. She didn't. She said she ran into the house, locked the doors, and hid, expecting him to come after her. She didn't have to tell me how scared she was. I knew. When I saw the shame in her eyes, I knew it was the right time to tell her. I told her that I was raped too. I didn't tell her any of the details, but I told her about the fear and the guilt and the shame I felt and I could see relief come over her. She wasn't alone. She had someone who understood exactly how she was feeling, and I did.

Then she told me something that surprised me, "I did what you said, Mama. I tried not to be afraid. I did everything he told me to do, and he brought me home, just like you said he would."

I had told my daughters so many things, but I didn't remember telling them that. If I did, then possibly those words may have saved her life. I held her in my arms so tight, and together we cried. She was alive and she was safe, and that's all that mattered. He could have killed her and thrown her in the field behind that barn. We would have never found her. As I held her, it crossed my mind that maybe what happened to me had happened for a reason and had prepared me for just this day.

My husband knew Kenneth. I didn't. I did, however, know who his brother was. While my husband was calling the police, I went to his closet and got his baseball bat. Without a word to anyone, I got into my car and drove to the auto repair shop where Kenneth worked. As soon as I drove in, he must have known who I was because he started running. He ran into another room and locked the door. I went after him and didn't see his brother come up behind me. He grabbed me and held my arms so I couldn't move.

"Let me go," I screamed as I fought him.

Finally he managed to calm me down enough to ask, "What has he done?"

"He raped my child." I could barely get the words out.

I kept fighting to break his hold on me. My intention was to bash his brother's brain in. I didn't care what happened to me. I was there to kill him, and I wasn't leaving until I did. When he saw that I couldn't move, Kenneth took off running to his truck and I yelled at him, "Go ahead and run. It doesn't matter where you run to. I'll find you and I'm going to kill you."

By the time I got home, a policeman was there, but he wasn't there just to find about Margaret. He was also there because Kenneth had driven straight to the sheriff's office and reported that I had attempted to assault him.

I explained to the officer, "I didn't go there to assault him. I went there to kill him, and I have every intention of doing it. So do what you have to." He warned me to stay away from Kenneth or I would be carried to jail.

His report read that Margaret was eighteen years old. She knew the man and got into his truck by her own will. Rape could not be reported. It didn't matter that she had the mind of a child; she was considered an adult and knew what she was doing.

Because of the sensitive nature of the case, the district attorney, a friend of mine, was called in. Kenneth was a grown man but had problems, and then the same term that was given to Uncle Tea was given to him. "He's not right," they said.

"What does that mean?" I screamed. "Because he's got mental issues, it's okay that he did what he did to my daughter? Is that what you're telling me?"

As much as they tried to explain it to me, I was having none of it. Yes, I wanted him punished, but more than that, I had to know that he couldn't hurt another child. Finally, because they couldn't arrest him, the agreement was made between my husband and me and his family that he would be sent away for two years to another state to live with relatives, but still that didn't satisfy me. I insisted that he wear a monitor around his ankle so his whereabouts could be traced. I had to be sure that he couldn't rape again. Kenneth was sent away immediately.

When the rape was told about in the newspaper, Margaret's name was not revealed. I had insisted on it. Finally, after all these years, it became clear to me why Mama never told anyone I was raped. I didn't want Margaret to be the butt of everyone's gossip, and I certainly didn't want anyone asking her questions about what happened. Everyone knew her and loved her, but people can still be cruel and are quick to place blame. It would take a long time for her to get over the rape, although I knew she never would, and as much as I wanted to help her work through it, I knew that only a doctor could. I got her into counseling immediately. I had to do everything I could to keep her from ending up like me.

After two years, Kenneth came back home. We were in the grocery store one day. Margaret always went to the magazine section while I shopped. Suddenly, she came running up to me and said, "Mama, he's here."

That's all it took. She didn't have to tell me who. I knew it was him. I went up and down every aisle until I found him, and I could tell right away that he was scared of me. Very simply, I told him that if I ever caught him anywhere in the vicinity of my daughter again, I would call the police.

Margaret has never gotten over the rape, but I never expected her to. All these years later, when she brings it up and wants to talk about it, we do. She would give anything to be married and have children like her sisters. She has been asked out on dates but always says, "No," and I hate to admit it, but I've never encouraged her. It doesn't matter how old she gets, she'll always have the mind of a young girl and I'll always have the role of her protector.

TELLING DADDY EVERYTHING

I was thirty-six years old when I decided to tell Daddy what happened. Mama had died just one year before. I don't know why, but even after I was married, I still couldn't talk to her about Kathy or the rapes. She was visibly aware that I had problems, and even after I was diagnosed with bipolar disorder, she wouldn't accept it. She insisted that there was nothing wrong with me.

When I decided to tell Daddy what happened to me, I started at the very first, when I was five years old, when Uncle Tea molested me. I was determined not to leave anything out, although I could see how uncomfortable he was. He didn't give me time to finish before he got up and walked to the window. He took his handkerchief out, wiped his eyes, and blew his nose. He was actually crying.

"Why didn't you tell somebody?" he said.

"That's the question I have for you, Daddy. Why couldn't I tell you what happened?"

He shot a look at me that I will never forget. "I'm sorry this happened to you, Molly, but don't you blame this on me!" he said. "You should have told someone so we could stop it. Tea raped another little girl. She almost died. If you had just told us, we could have prevented that."

And there it was. His concern wasn't for me. It was for the other girl, and he was pretty much saying, "It's your fault he hurt her."

Although the tears welled up, I was determined that I was not going to cry. I would get through this no matter what.

I proceeded to talk to him about Kathy's death and how they didn't tell me what happened to her or where she went. I told him about the day of her funeral and his reaction when I broke her angel.

"I didn't do that," he insisted.

"You did, Daddy, and it probably seems like a small, insignificant thing to you, but it devastated me. None of you knew how much I loved Kathy and none of you cared what her death did to me. I knew how bad you and Mama were hurting, and so I was careful to hide my hurt from you. I wish you had cared that much about me."

That's when he got angry. "Why are you bringing all this up?" he said.

"I'm sick, Daddy, and I'm not going to get better until I understand things. I have to let go of this guilt and anger I'm holding inside. Who else am I suppose to tell?"

Again he turned his back to me.

I went on to tell him about Mr. Thompson, the milkman. At first, I don't think he believed me, but he remembered Mr. Thompson and called him by his first name. "He was such a nice guy," he said. "That's hard to believe." He seemed more amazed at what this nice guy had done than what he had done to me.

"He stalked me for four years, Daddy, from the time I was ten until I turned fourteen. I thought I'd go crazy."

"Why didn't you tell us?" he demanded.

"I couldn't," I said. "I was afraid you'd think it was my fault."

"It wasn't," was all he said.

He didn't give me a chance to finish, and there was so much more to tell him. He turned and looked at me. "Who knows about this? Who have you told?"

"Just my doctor and Bobby," I told him. "No one else knows."

"Don't tell anyone else," he demanded. "All it will do is give people something to talk about, and it will only embarrass our family. All of this happened a long time ago. You need to just forget about it."

And then he walked across the room to the door to leave, but before he could, I told him, "You want to know why I didn't tell you, Daddy?

Because it would have given you and Mama more to fight about, and I didn't want you to fight because of me."

He didn't answer me. He turned and walked out the door. The understanding and the sympathy I had hoped for was not there. Just as I had suspected all along, he blamed me, not for what happened but because I didn't tell. I can only rationalize it by thinking that he wasn't hearing this from a little girl but from a grown woman. That day, I cried harder than I had ever cried in my life, but something also happened to me. I felt this sudden release inside. The guilt and the shame I had carried in my heart for so many years was gone. I finally knew that what happened was not my fault, none of it. My instinct had been right all along. There was no one to help me. I had survived all these things because of my own willpower, and just maybe God had played a part in it too. He had been listening all along, and he had answered my prayers.

My grandmother, Mammie, died when she was eighty-seven years old. When she lay on her deathbed in the hospital and had very little time left to live, the family was taking turns going in to see her for the last time. I was waiting in the hallway for my turn, when daddy came out and said to me, "Don't you go in and confess to Mammie what happened to you. It's not the time or the place." I couldn't believe my ears and couldn't respond. He actually called it a confession. Whether he meant to say that word or not, I still don't know. I looked at him almost in pity and that's what I felt. I had tried to explain to him what happened with Uncle Tea, but he just didn't get that I was five years old when it happened. I wasn't an adult who could stop what happened. Rather than try to talk to him, I just dropped it. Mammie never knew what happened and if I didn't tell her all those years, why would I tell her on her death bed. What I resented the most was the fact that he thought I was that dumb or unfeeling.

No child should ever have to go through what I did, but they do every day. There's not a day that goes by when the news doesn't report that some child has been kidnapped, raped, and most of the time, murdered. And what about those children like me, who it happened to but who never told? They may not have died, but their lives were destroyed just the same, and probably, just like me, they have lived with the guilt that somehow they caused it. All that I can hope for is that, unlike me, someone cared enough about them to know that something was wrong. They found out what was happening and they saved them.

It took sixteen years before my mental problems surfaced, and when the bipolar disorder took me over, it's as though another person buried deep inside of me took over my body and my life. The plans and experiences I had dreamed of were taken from me, and finally when that person left, my chance to fulfill those dreams was over. I lost my husband, my children, my friends, and the job I loved. No one understood what was happening to me, but neither did I. I saw myself doing crazy things, things completely the opposite of the person I am, but I couldn't stop it. That person inside of me dominated my thoughts and my actions. They were embarrassing and humiliating actions that I had no control over, and I wish my family understood this, but they don't and they never will.

It took years before the doctor could find medication that would control the bouts of depression that would spiral into mania. I've worked very hard to gain my family's trust and love back and slowly but surely they are coming back. For all those years, though, I lost part of my life, and I'll never get that back. Maybe the disorder is genetic, but I'll always know in my heart that my childhood caused the breakdown, and I'll always blame my parents for it.

One of the things I remember asking Daddy that day he came to see me was, "What kind of child was I?"

"You were always quiet. You never talked. You never seemed happy," he said. "It was as though you had no personality, no emotion." But he was wrong. I was filled with emotion. I just kept it buried deep inside of me.

MY LIFE AS A BIPOLAR

The first signs of the bipolar illness actually presented itself when I was twenty-eight years old. Immediately following high school graduation, I started college at Middle Tennessee State University in Murfreesboro, Tennessee, although I had no money to go to college and no offers from my dad to help me. I had to borrow the money from a bank at a high interest rate, and because of the expense, I was determined to make the best grades possible with the hope that my hard work and sacrifice would pay off in the end. Eventually, because of the mounting expenses, I had to drop out of the university and get a full-time job. I went to school at the local community college at night and picked up a few classes I needed for my degree.

When I was twenty years old, I married Bobby. I continued to work a full-time job, took classes part-time, and added a child into the mix. My life was very busy, and because of that, I stopped thinking so much about the past. Everything that had happened was always with me, however, right there in the back of my mind, always haunting me.

Finally my ten years of hard work paid off. Graduation with a degree in business education was just a semester away. I had two children by then, six years and three years old, and I was pregnant with my third child. She was born in November. My student teaching, my last semester, started in January.

I don't know exactly what happened after she was born, but

everything started falling apart. Two small children, a new baby, a part-time job, and student teaching took its toll on me.

I know now that what I experienced was probably post-traumatic stress syndrome caused by childbirth. Whatever it was, it was devastating. I went into full-blown depression. I had to quit my part-time job, I couldn't take care of my children, and two weeks into my student teaching, I had to drop out. "Just four more weeks and you'll have your degree" was what everyone told me. "You can do this." As bad as I wanted it, my body and my brain would not cooperate. No one could believe that I was dropping out, mostly me, but I knew it just wasn't in my reach, not at that time.

I was humiliated and embarrassed and was harder on myself than they ever could be. For a while, in the back of my mind, however, I had sensed that something was going to happen that wasn't going to be good. Simple daily tasks were becoming impossible for me. The two weeks when I did the student teaching were awful. I would go to sleep as soon as I sat down at my desk, and the teacher I was working with wasn't happy with me at all. My confidence and my self-worth dropped to nothing. I had gotten to where I couldn't concentrate, couldn't sleep, and was unable to prepare for lessons the next day. Life had finally caught up with me. My body and my mind froze up completely.

The very day I dropped out, I sat down in my rocking chair, and for the next three months all I did was rock. My mother and my mother-in-law had to come every day and take care of my children. I knew something awful had happened to me, and as much as I wanted to come out of it, I couldn't. So I withdrew inside myself. I couldn't even carry on a simple conversation.

One day, Bob, my father-in-law, who had been more of a father to me than my own dad, came to the house, pulled a chair up, and sat right in front of me.

"I know how you like antiques," he said. "I bought you one. I put it in the garage along with a refinishing kit. When you feel up to it, I want you to bring it back to life," he said.

I wasn't able to respond. He kissed me on my forehead and left. For days, all I thought about was that antique sitting in my garage, and as much as I wanted to see it, I couldn't make myself get up and go out there. I just continued rocking.

Finally, after two more weeks, I came out of that rocking chair. I started playing with my children and helping with their daily care. The next thing I did was venture out to the garage to see what Bob had bought me. It was an antique chest of drawers, but there was no way to tell what the wood was because of the thick, brown paint smeared on it. I couldn't wait to attack it; however, I didn't start with the refinishing for a while. There were too many other things I needed to catch up on first. For that three months, my life had disappeared. I was still fighting the depression but knew that if I tried hard enough, it would go away; and it did, without the aid of medication. I brought myself out of it, but it was a tough battle.

As soon as I got back on my feet, my husband immediately took me to the doctor, and he diagnosed me as having a nervous condition. What he really meant was a nervous breakdown. I knew it was true and it had been long overdue. He prescribed Xanax for me to take, which was probably the worst thing he could have done. I did, however, start feeling better, and because I felt so good, I wouldn't stop taking it. I didn't go back to work until eight months later, and by then I felt like I was on top of things again. I started a new job, my children were settled in school and day care, and life was good. My education was over, however. I knew that. I had so much education debt that it would take years to pay it off. Any hopes of finishing my degree were too far in the distance to even think about. All the hard work I had done had gone down the drain. When I got my last grades in the mail, it showed my grade average as a 3.98, an almost perfect score, but I was disappointed that it wasn't a 4.0 average. I had made nothing but As and a few scattered Bs all the way through college. One of the things my childhood experiences had instilled in me was the need for perfection. Nothing else would do. I had to be the best at everything I did. Only then would I have approval. As always, I made it harder on myself than anyone else could.

From there on, my life went straight downhill. As much as Dr. J. tried to find a combination of drugs that would control the depression and the sudden bouts of mania, it just didn't seem that there was one. While I went to him, I was probably prescribed ten to twelve different medications. Every time I seemed to be doing better, he would change my medicine and try a newly released drug, and with every drug, there were different side effects.

I continued to see Dr. J. for eight years and for eight years he prescribed every medication he could for bipolar disorder but nothing seemed to work. Finally my husband got fed up. I don't know what was said between them, but Dr. J. dropped me as his patient. I had to start all over with a new doctor and new drugs. The periods of depression that would spiral into mania were so bad that I spent time in three more mental hospitals. After ten long years, I finally went to a doctor at Vanderbilt Hospital. I spent three weeks in the psychiatric hospital there. The doctor prescribed two drugs, Lamictal and Seroquel, and my condition leveled out completely and has stayed that way for eight years now.

One thing that my family did when my illness would cycle out of control was accuse me of not taking my medication, and it did me no good to contradict them. Truthfully, I feel that I never wavered from taking my medication, although I could have when I was manic. Mania is the greatest feeling in the world, and you'll do anything to hold onto it. I'm sure it could be compared to being high on cocaine. It was the only time I felt good about myself and felt that nothing in my life could go bad. I was just high on life, and as I've said before, I was so happy just to be me. The only problem is that your body won't allow you to be manic for long. Eventually you have to crash, and all you can hope for is that someone's there to help you get through it. I had Bobby to help me. The two medicines that were prescribed to control the depression and the mania worked well together, and for several years I was completely leveled out.

When my children had grown into adulthood and the last one had turned twenty-one and graduated from college, Bobby divorced me for a young girl who was the age of my oldest daughter. She was thirty years old. He was fifty-nine. When he left, I fell completely apart. I went into the deepest of depressions. I wandered around the house from room to room, crying all the while. I rarely took a bath or cleaned up after myself. Finally, one day I decided it needed to end and I attempted suicide. I emptied every bottle of medicine in the house into a large bowl and I swallowed handfuls at a time with water. I didn't get through the whole bowl before I passed out. Luckily, it wasn't long before one of my daughters came to visit and found me passed out on the bedroom floor. I was rushed to the hospital, and my stomach was pumped. I was transferred to a mental hospital where I stayed for a week. When they released me, I wasn't ready. I had to go back and I stayed for two more weeks. I should have died, but once again I pulled through it. I have to believe that God intervened and saved me that day, just as he always had.

They say it's devastating when your spouse dies, but I have to think it's harder with a divorce. I had loved Bobby so much and still did, and although he was still alive, he was out of my reach. I couldn't hold him anymore and tell him how much I loved him, and I didn't have him to hold me and tell me that everything was going to be alright. It was hard for me to carry on the smallest of everyday functions. I would see him from time to time, and she was always with him. Bobby and I were married for thirty years, and in five seconds, with the words "I'm leaving you," my life dropped out from under me.

I still see him from time to time, but he's like a stranger to me; like someone I never knew. He left eight years ago. It took the first two year for me to come out of the depression. He was the only person in my life who had ever really loved me, and made me feel safe. Somehow, I knew that whatever happened, he was always there to lift me back up when I fell. I guess my illness just got to be too much for him, and although I regret it, I do understand why he left.

Two of my daughters have married, and I have four grandchildren now. Margaret still lives with me and provides me with more love than I could ever ask for.

My life is simple now and uncomplicated, and it's been eight years since I have had a bout of depression or mania. Because of the illness, I lost my family for a while. My children couldn't handle my illness and didn't come around me, but I have never blamed them. Bipolar disorder is a tough illness and one you have to stay on top of every day of your life, and I try very hard to, not only for myself, but for them too.

I'm so thankful to have my family back and so thankful that my chemical imbalance is leveled out, but every day I know that it's possible for me to slip back into it, and every day I pray to God to be with me. I ask him to keep the demons away, if only for that day. I accused God of not listening to the many prayers I sent him during my childhood. I can see now that he did answer them, maybe not in the way I hoped for, and maybe not in the short period of time I hoped for, but I do know that he was always watching over me.

At the beginning of my story, I wrote that writing my memories down in journals didn't help me. I was wrong. After I wrote the last journal, I put it away for a while, trying to decide if I wanted to publish it or not. One day, not too long ago, I sat down and read the journals from cover to cover just to check for errors. I cried a lot. It's almost like it wasn't me who all those things happened to. It was another little girl, and day after day after day, she was going through a living hell and had no one to turn to. I have to say now that the journals were a true discovery for me. I had told Dr. J. everything there was to tell, but seeing it written down and reading it has actually been the best thing I was ever advised to do. In a way, it has given me a sense of closure. Yes, all of it happened, but it's over now. Throughout my life, I have spent most of my time trying to hide the demons that haunt me from everyone and worrying about what people think of me but nothing can be done about what happened. I have to let it go. There's too much of life left to live.

Helen Keller once wrote: "Character cannot be developed in ease and quiet. Only through experience of trial and suffering can the soul be strengthened, ambition inspired, and success achieved."

What I went through as a child was nightmare after nightmare. But I feel that I've finally come out on top and with a knowledge about life that most people will never possess. I'm strong now and I'm prepared for anything that comes my way, be it good or bad.

Over these many years, I have watched and listened to reports every day of children being kidnapped, raped, and murdered. Those who survived more than likely ended up like me, scarred for life. I wish that my story would help those children going through the same things and also those children who, so far, are untouched. I always go back to the same fact. There are people who are supposed to protect us in our young lives. They are responsible for what happens to us. Why don't they take that responsibility as seriously as it needs to be taken?

After I wrote my journals, Dr. J. asked me what my message would be if I were to publish them. I think my message is this:

There's always going to be someone in your life who will try to hurt you in body, in mind, or in your heart. The question is: how will you deal with that hurt? You can do as I did and keep it to yourself out of fear of someone hurting you or out of fear of someone finding out what happened. You can hold that fear inside of you forever and let it slowly consume you, or you can put your trust in someone and ask for help. If your parents have done their job and have instilled that trust in you, then you are very lucky and you have to go to them for help. If you're not that lucky, then I want you to know that there is someone out there who will believe you and do everything in their power to help you. You have to search them out. No matter what happens or what you are afraid will happen, it can't be any worse than carrying that hurt inside of you and letting it slowly destroy you. Don't let another person take your life from you. And no matter what, know this: you did nothing wrong.

Bipolar disorder is a nightmare. If you have it, you need to know that you did not cause it. It is a chemical imbalance in your brain. There is no cure for it. All you can do is try to control it. The most important factors in dealing with the illness are having the right doctor and ensuring that the doctor is prescribing the right medications for you. It might take a while for these two things to come together. After being on a drug for at least two to three weeks, I usually knew whether or not that specific drug was going to work for me. If I felt like it wasn't controlling the depression or the mania, I was back at the doctor's office immediately. The doctor can do all he can to help you control the illness, but it comes down to you. You have to take your medication. The depression is terrible, but the mania is worse. Not only can it destroy you, but it destroys your family, your friends, and your very existence.

I have a friend who is also bipolar. When she gets balanced out and feels like herself, she thinks she doesn't need the medication anymore. She stops taking it, and although I try to talk to her, she doesn't listen. She always slips and either goes back into depression or into mania and has to be hospitalized.

Having been diagnosed as bipolar years ago, I know that the one thing that can work against my medications is stress, so I try not to worry about the little things. I try to keep my life as calm as possible. The ups and the downs and the states of mania and depression were not only hard on me mentally, but they were just as hard on me physically. Sometimes I have to think it was harder on my husband and children than it was on me, and no matter how much I wish, I can't wish it away. The only thing I can do is try to help them understand me and what goes on in my head.

MAMA AND DADDY

Everything I have written about Mama and Daddy make them seem like they were probably low-class, uneducated, self-centered people, but it's just the opposite. Both Mama and Daddy had a high school education, they were both hard-working, middle-class people, and they were loving parents. They just had a dysfunctional relationship, and because of that, it extended to my brothers and me.

Daddy had a good relationship with my brothers. He just didn't seem to know what to do with me, and I never saw an affectionate side to Daddy, except with Kathy.

Mama loved me. I was always sure of that. But I don't think she knew what to do with me either. Mama's parents died when she was two years old. She had six sisters who were older than her but none of them were adults; and they could not take care of a baby. So she was placed in a Catholic orphanage and raised under the strict rule of the Dominican nuns. I have to believe that Mama did the best she could with the limited knowledge she possessed, and the subject of sex was probably taught to her in a negative way. So that was all she knew. Whatever the reason, I know she did the best she could do.

There is one thing I'm sure of, however. Although Mama and Daddy argued and fussed all the time, there were times when I could see true, honest love between them. It was there whether they wanted to admit it or not, but after Kathy's death, I never saw it again, not even when they got remarried. They had lost something that couldn't be replaced, and no matter how hard they tried, neither one of them ever got over her death. From the day Kathy died, I knew better than to bring her up to Mama. Her eyes would water up immediately, and I sensed the sadness I was causing her.

As for Daddy, I never discussed Kathy with him either except that day I called him to come see me. Even then when I mentioned her name, there was sadness in his eyes and in his voice. I never knew exactly what kind of cancer Kathy died of. I remember Kathy telling Daddy, when he found her knotted up under his bed, "My belly hurts." It wasn't until just recently that I brought her up again because I was trying to complete my journals. He had called me on January 20 to wish me a happy birthday, just as he always did, if he happened to remember. I always had to tell him, "January 20 is Kathy's birthday, Daddy. Mine is January 28." He would always laugh it off, but his voice would change and I would sense such a sadness in him. When he called me to wish me a happy birthday this last time, I reminded him of how old Kathy would be now (fifty-four years old), but it seems like she died just yesterday. At first I hesitated but finally decided to ask him what kind of cancer Kathy had. Even after all these years, I had never known. All he said was, "It started in her kidneys," and he changed the subject.

As an adult and a parent, I have had friends over the years whose children have either died by illness or have died in an automobile accident. Every day I see them struggle trying to make life for themselves and their children as normal and as happy as they possibly can, but there's a sadness in them too, the same sadness I saw in my parents and the same sadness I still feel, even after all this time. It never goes away.

So whatever I have written and whatever I have said, I would never want anyone to assume that Mama and Daddy were bad parents. I truly believe that they did the best they could with the knowledge and skills of parenting that they had.

When I talked to Daddy all those years ago and asked him what kind of child I was, he had said "You were always quiet. You never talked. You never seemed happy. It was as though you had no personality, no emotion." I would like to think that I was a happy child before everything started happening to me, a child who was loved, a child who was able to give love in return. As children, we have no way of knowing what road in life we're supposed to take. We depend on our parents to shape that path for us, and all we can hope for is that they do it well.